Table of Conter

Operations and Algebraic Thinking

▶ **Represent and solve problems involving addition and subtraction.**

▶ **Understand and apply properties of operations and the relationship between addition and subtraction.**

▶ **Add and subtract within 20.**

▶ **Work with addition and subtraction equations.**

Number and Operations in Base Ten

▶ **Extend the counting sequence.**

▶ **Understand place value.**

▶ **Use place value understanding and properties of operations to add and subtract.**

Measurement and Data

▶ **Measure lengths indirectly and by iterating length units.**

▶ **Tell and write time.**

▶ **Represent and interpret data.**

Geometry

▶ **Reason with shapes and their attributes.**

Introduction

Core Standards for Math offers two-page lessons for every content standard in the *Common Core State Standards for Mathematics*. The first page of each lesson introduces the concept or skill being taught by providing step-by-step instruction and modeling and checks students' understanding through open-ended practice items. The second page includes multiple-choice practice items as well as problem-solving items.

Common Core State Standards for Mathematics: Content Standards

Content Standards define what students should understand and be able to do. These standards are organized into clusters of related standards to emphasize mathematical connections. Finally, domains represent larger groups of related standards. At the elementary (K–6) level, there are ten content domains. Each grade addresses four or five domains. The table below shows how the domains are placed across Grades K–6.

Domains	Grade Levels						
	K	1	2	3	4	5	6
Counting and Cardinality (CC)	•						
Operations and Algebraic Thinking (OA)	•	•	•	•	•	•	
Numbers and Operations in Base Ten (NBT)	•	•	•	•	•	•	
Measurement and Data (MD)	•	•	•	•	•	•	
Geometry (G)	•	•	•	•	•	•	•
Numbers and Operations—Fractions (NF)				•	•	•	
Ratios and Proportional Relationships (RP)							•
The Number System (NS)							•
Expressions and Equations (EE)							•
Statistics and Probability (SP)							•

The lessons in **Core Standards for Math** are organized by content standard. The content standard is listed at the top right-hand corner of each page. The entire text of the standards is provided on pages 251–254. The lesson objective listed below the content standard number indicates what part of the standard is emphasized in the lesson. You may choose to have students complete all the lessons for a particular standard or select lessons based on the more focused objectives.

Lesson 1

COMMON CORE STANDARD CC.1.OA.1
Lesson Objective: Use pictures to "add to" and find sums.

Algebra • Use Pictures to Add To

3 cows   and   2 more cows   __5__ cows.

Draw circles around the animals added to the group. Write how many.

1.

3 cats   and   4 more cats   _____ cats

2.

2 bees   and   2 more bees   _____ bees

3.

5 dogs   and   1 more dog   _____ dogs

Core Standards for Math, Grade 1

1. How many dogs?

4 dogs   and   5 more dogs

   ○ 6   ○ 7

   ○ 8   ○ 9

3. How many fish?

3 fish   and   2 more fish

   ○ 6   ○ 5

   ○ 4   ○ 3

2. How many birds?

4 birds   and   2 more birds

   ○ 5

   ○ 6

   ○ 7

   ○ 8

4. How many cats?

3 cats   and   4 more cats

   ○ 5

   ○ 6

   ○ 7

   ○ 8

PROBLEM SOLVING REAL WORLD

5. There are 2 rabbits. 5 rabbits join
them. How many rabbits are there now?

There are _____ rabbits.

Lesson 2

COMMON CORE STANDARD CC.1.OA.1

Lesson Objective: Use concrete objects to solve "adding to" addition problems.

Model Adding To

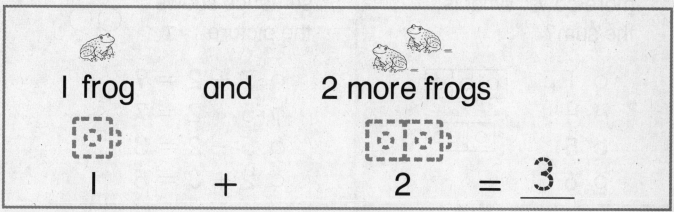

I frog   and   2 more frogs

1   +   2   =   3

Use ▢ to show adding to. Draw the ▢.
Write the sum.

1. 3 horses and 4 more horses

3   +   4   = ___

2. I bee and I more bee

1   +   1   = ___

3. 4 cows and I more cow

4   +   1   = ___

Core Standards for Math, Grade 1

1. Rey saw 3 cows and 2 more cows. What is the sum?

   ○ 1
   ○ 4
   ○ 5
   ○ 6

3. Which number sentence shows the picture?

   ○ $7 + 2 = 9$
   ○ $5 + 2 = 7$
   ○ $5 - 2 = 3$
   ○ $2 + 3 = 5$

2. Tina read 4 books. Then she read 3 more books. What is the sum?

   ○ 2
   ○ 5
   ○ 6
   ○ 7

4. What is the sum of 4 and 4?

   ○ 8
   ○ 6
   ○ 4
   ○ 2

PROBLEM SOLVING REAL WORLD

Use the picture to help you complete the addition sentences. Write each sum.

5. _____  + _____ = _____ in all

6. _____  + _____ = _____ in all

Name _____

Lesson 3

COMMON CORE STANDARD CC.1.OA.1

Lesson Objective: Use concrete objects to solve "putting together" addition problems.

Model Putting Together

Use 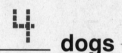 to add two groups.
Put the groups together to
find how many.

There are 3 brown dogs.

There is 1 white dog.

How many dogs are there?

$3 + 1 = 4$

__4__ dogs

Use ⬤ ◯ to solve. Draw to show your work.
Write how many.

1. There are 4 black bears and
   3 brown bears. How many
   bears are there?

   _____ bears

   $4 + 3 = $ _____

2. There are 6 red flowers and
   2 white flowers. How many
   flowers are there?

   _____ flowers

   $6 + 2 = $ _____

1. There are 2 large flowers and 1 small flower. How many flowers are there?

2 + 1 = _____

○ 4   ○ 3

○ 2   ○ 1

3. There are 4 red flowers and 2 yellow flowers. How many flowers are there?

4 + 2 = _____

○ 3   ○ 5

○ 6   ○ 7

2. There are 3 red grapes and 6 green grapes. How many grapes are there?

○ 9   ○ 8

○ 7   ○ 6

4. There are 3 black fish and 2 blue fish. How many fish are there?

○ 1   ○ 3

○ 4   ○ 5

PROBLEM SOLVING

5. Write your own addition story problem.

_____

- -

_____

_____

- -

_____

Name _____

Lesson 4

COMMON CORE STANDARD CC.1.OA.1
Lesson Objective: Solve adding to and
putting together situations using the strategy
make a model.

Problem Solving • Model Addition

Rico has 3 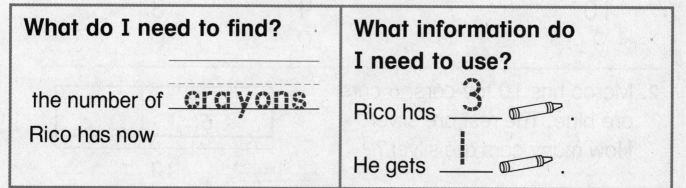. Then he gets 1 more 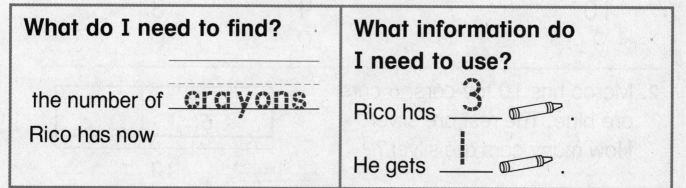.
How many 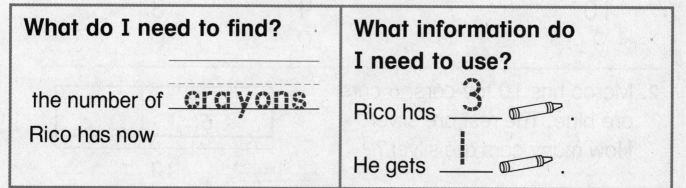 does he have now?

Unlock the Problem

What do I need to find?	**What information do I need to use?**
the number of **crayons** Rico has now	Rico has **3** . He gets **1** .

Show how to solve the problem.

3	1

4

$3 + 1 =$ ___

Read the problem. Use the bar model to solve.

Complete the model and the number sentence.

1. There are 5 birds flying.
   Then 3 more birds join them.
   How many birds are flying now?

5	3

$5 + 3 =$ ___   ___

1. 7 ladybugs are walking. 3 more ladybugs walk with them. How many ladybugs are walking now?

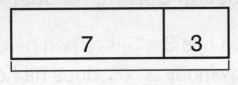

| 7 | 3 |

___

10 ○   7 ○   4 ○   3 ○

2. Marco has 10 toy cars. 6 cars are blue. The rest are silver. How many cars are silver?

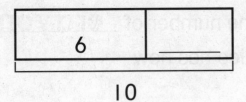

| 6 | ___ |

10

16 ○   10 ○   6 ○   4 ○

3. 6 bees are in a hive. 3 more bees fly in. How many bees are in the hive now?

9 ○   8 ○   7 ○   3 ○

4. There are 4 birds. Then other birds join them. Now there are 7 birds. How many birds joined them? Draw a model to solve. Write a number sentence.

Name _____

Lesson **5**

COMMON CORE STANDARD CC.1.OA.1
Lesson Objective: Model and record all
the ways to put together numbers within 10.

Algebra • Put Together
Numbers to 10

You can use to model ways to make 7.

○○○○○○● $6 + \underline{1} = 7$

○○○○○●● $5 + \underline{2} = 7$

Use . Draw to show how to make 7.
Complete the addition sentences.

1. ○○○○

   $4 + \underline{} = 7$

2. ○○○

   $3 + \underline{} = 7$

3. ○○

   $2 + \underline{} = 7$

4. ○

   $1 + \underline{} = 7$

© Houghton Mifflin Harcourt Publishing Company

9

Core Standards for Math, Grade 1

1. Which shows a way to make 5?

   ○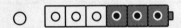

   ○

   ○

   ○

3. Which is **not** a way to make 10?

   ○ 0 + 1
   ○ 3 + 7
   ○ 5 + 5
   ○ 8 + 2

2. Which shows a way to make 8?

   ○

   ○

   ○

   ○

4. Which is **not** a way to make 9?

   ○ 8 + 1
   ○ 7 + 2
   ○ 6 + 3
   ○ 5 + 5

5. Color  to show a way to make 6. Write two addition sentences to go with your picture.

_____

_____

COMMON CORE STANDARD CC.1.OA.1
Lesson Objective: Use pictures to show
"taking from" and find differences.

Use Pictures to Show Taking From

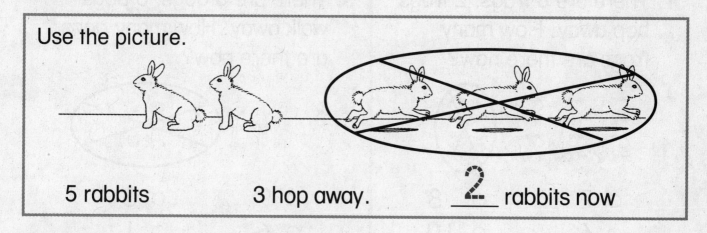

Use the picture.

5 rabbits   3 hop away.   __2__ rabbits now

Write how many there are now.

I.

8 birds   4 fly away.   _____ birds now

2.

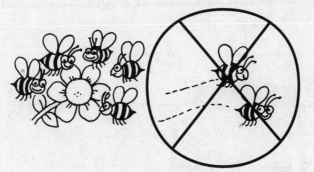

7 bees   2 fly away.   _____ bees now

1. There are 8 frogs. 2 frogs hop away. How many frogs are there now?

- ○ 2
- ○ 8
- ○ 6
- ○ 10

3. There are 6 dogs. 3 dogs walk away. How many dogs are there now?

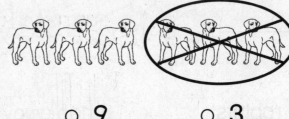

- ○ 9
- ○ 3
- ○ 6
- ○ 1

2. There are 7 cats. 3 cats run away. How many cats are there now?

- ○ 4
- ○ 10
- ○ 7
- ○ 11

4. There are 5 fish. 4 fish swim away. How many fish are there now?

- ○ 9
- ○ 2
- ○ 3
- ○ 1

PROBLEM SOLVING  REAL WORLD

Solve.

5. There are 7 birds. 2 birds fly away.
   How many birds are there now?

   _____ birds

Name _____

Lesson 7

COMMON CORE STANDARD CC.1.OA.1

Lesson Objective: Use concrete objects to solve "taking from" subtraction problems.

Model Taking From

Circle the part you take from the group.
Then cross it out.

3 dogs   2 dogs run away.   _____ dog now

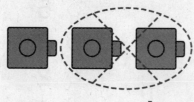

$$3 - 2 = \underline{1}$$

Circle the part you take from the group.
Then cross it out. Write the difference.

1.   4 goats   2 goats walk away.   _____ goats now

$$4 - 2 = \underline{}$$

2.   6 ants   3 ants walk away.   _____ ants now

$$6 - 3 = \underline{}$$

1. What is the difference?

7 − 3 = _____

- ○ 3
- ○ 4
- ○ 7
- ○ 10

3. What is the difference?

- ○ 7
- ○ 5
- ○ 3
- ○ 2

2. What is the difference?

10 − 8 = _____

- ○ 2
- ○ 7
- ○ 9
- ○ 16

4. What is the difference?

- ○ 2
- ○ 5
- ○ 10
- ○ 15

PROBLEM SOLVING REAL WORLD

Draw  to solve. Complete
the subtraction sentence.

5. There are 8 fish.
4 fish swim away.
How many fish
are there now?

___ − ___ = ___

___ fish

Core Standards for Math, Grade 1

Name _____

Lesson 8

COMMON CORE STANDARD CC.1.OA.1

Lesson Objective: Use concrete objects to solve "taking apart" subtraction problems.

Model Taking Apart

You can use ◯ to **subtract**.
Sam has 6 cars. 4 cars are red.
The rest are yellow.
How many cars are yellow?

_2_ cars are yellow.

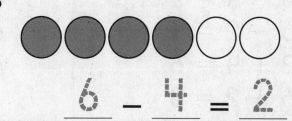

$$6 - 4 = 2$$

Use ◯ to solve. Color. Write the number sentence and how many.

1. There are 5 books.
   1 book is red. The rest are yellow. How many books are yellow?

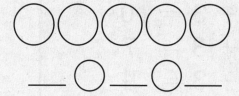

___ ◯ ___ ◯ ___

____ yellow books

2. There are 6 blocks.
   3 blocks are small.
   The rest are big.
   How many blocks are big?

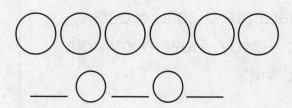

___ ◯ ___ ◯ ___

____ big blocks

1. There are 6 snakes. 2 snakes are green. The rest are brown. How many snakes are brown?

   ○ $6 - 4 = 2$
   ○ $6 - 2 = 4$
   ○ $2 + 4 = 6$
   ○ $6 + 2 = 8$

2. There are 7 tents. 3 tents are blue. The rest are orange. How many tents are orange?

   ○ $7 + 3 = 10$
   ○ $4 + 3 = 7$
   ○ $7 - 3 = 4$
   ○ $7 - 4 = 3$

3. There are 5 snails. 4 snails are small. The rest are big. How many snails are big?

   ○ 3
   ○ 2
   ○ 1
   ○ 0

4. There are 8 trees. 3 trees are pines. The rest are oaks. How many trees are oaks?

   ○ 5
   ○ 4
   ○ 3
   ○ 2

PROBLEM SOLVING  REAL WORLD

Solve. Draw a model to explain.

5. There are 8 cats. 6 cats walk away. How many cats are left?

_____ cats left

Name _____

Lesson 9

COMMON CORE STANDARD CC.1.OA.1

Lesson Objective: Solve taking from and taking apart subtraction problems using the strategy *make a model*.

Problem Solving • Model Subtraction

There were 9 bugs on a rock. 7 bugs ran away.
How many bugs are on the rock now?

What do I need to find?	**What information do I need to use?**
how many __bugs__ on the rock now	_9_ bugs on a rock _7_ bugs ran away

Show how to solve the problem.

7	2

9

$9 - 7 = \underline{2}$

Read the problem. Use the model to solve.

Complete the model and the number sentence.

1. There are 5 birds. 1 bird is big. The rest are small.
   How many birds are small?

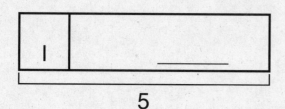

1	___

5

$5 - 1 = \underline{}$

1. A shop had some fish in a tank. 4 fish were sold. Then there were 5 fish left in the tank. How many fish did the shop have?

   ○ 1   ○ 8
   ○ 3   ○ 9

2. There are 10 hats. 4 hats are blue. The rest are red. How many hats are red?

   ○ 10   ○ 5
   ○ 6   ○ 4

3. Kenny has 7 pets. 3 are turtles. The rest are birds. How many birds does Kenny have?

   ○ 10   ○ 4
   ○ 5   ○ 3

4. There were 9 girls at the party. Some girls left. Then there were 3 girls. How many girls left?

   ○ 6   ○ 4
   ○ 5   ○ 3

5. Nell has 7 books. 5 are picture books. The rest are chapter books. How many chapter books does Nell have? Complete the model and number sentence.

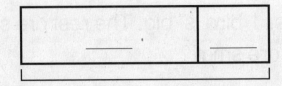

_____ ◯ _____ ◯ _____

Name _____

Lesson 10

COMMON CORE STANDARD CC.1.OA.1

Lesson Objective: Model and compare groups to show the meaning of subtraction.

Subtract to Compare

You can use 🔲 to show the bar model.

8 ⬤⬤⬤⬤⬤⬤⬤⬤

6 ◯◯◯◯◯◯

Andy has 8 balloons.
Jill has 6 balloons.
How many more balloons
does Andy have than Jill?

| 8 |
| 6 | | 2 |

_____ more balloons

$\underline{8} - \underline{6} = \underline{2}$

Read the problem. Use the bar model to solve. Write the number sentence. Then write how many.

1. Bo has 6 rocks.
   Jen has 4 rocks.
   How many more rocks
   does Bo have than Jen?

6 ⬤⬤⬤⬤⬤⬤

4 ◯◯◯◯

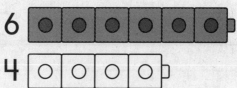

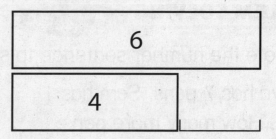

| 6 |
| 4 | |

_____ more rocks

___ − ___ = ___

Core Standards for Math, Grade 1

1. Eli has 5 pens. Hana has 8 pens.
   How many fewer pens does Eli have?

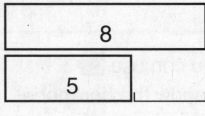

2
○

3
○

4
○

5
○

2. Kim has 4 shells. Josh has 6 shells.
   How many more shells does
   Josh have than Kim?

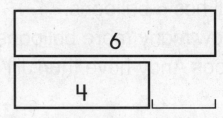

10
○

5
○

3
○

2
○

3. Erin has 4 pennies. Ryan has
   10 pennies. How many fewer
   pennies does Erin have than Ryan?

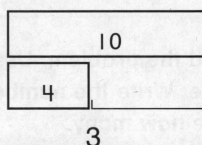

6
○

5
○

4
○

3
○

PROBLEM SOLVING

Complete the number sentence to solve.

4. Maya has 7 pens. Sam has 1
   pen. How many more pens
   does Maya have than Sam?

   _____ – _____ = _____

   _____ more pens

Lesson 11

COMMON CORE STANDARD CC.1.OA.1

Lesson Objective: Model and record all of the ways to take apart numbers within 10.

Algebra • Take Apart Numbers

You can use ⬤ to take apart 6.

Circle the part you take away.

Then cross it out.

$6 - 5 = \underline{1}$

$6 - 4 = \underline{2}$

Use ⬤ to take apart 6. Circle the part you take away. Then cross it out. **Complete the subtraction sentence.**

1.  $6 - 3 = \underline{}$

2.  $6 - 2 = \underline{}$

3. ○○○○○○ $6 - 1 = \underline{}$

4. ○○○○○○ $6 - 0 = \underline{}$

1. Which number sentence comes next in the pattern?

□□□□□□□ $7 - 0 = 7$

□□□□□□⊠ $7 - 1 = 6$

□□□□□⊠⊠ $7 - 2 = 5$

□□□□⊠⊠⊠ $7 - 3 = 4$

○ $7 - 5 = 2$
○ $7 - 4 = 3$
○ $7 - 3 = 4$
○ $7 - 2 = 5$

2. Which shows a way to take apart 8?

○ $8 + 1 = 9$
○ $9 - 1 = 8$
○ $10 - 2 = 8$
○ $8 - 6 = 2$

PROBLEM SOLVING  REAL WORLD

Solve.

3. Joe has 9 marbles. He gives them all to his sister. How many marbles does he have now?

_____ marbles

Name _____

Problem Solving • Use Subtraction Strategies

Lara has 15 crackers. She gives some of them away. She has 8 left. How many crackers does she give away?

Unlock the Problem

What do I need to find?	**What information do I need to use?**
how many ⌐crackers¬	Lara has __15__ crackers.
Lara gives away	Lara has __8__ crackers left.

Show how to solve the problem.

◯ ◯ ◯ ◯ ◯ ◯ ◯ ◯ ⦅◯ ◯ ◯ ◯ ◯ ◯ ◯⦆

Lara gives away __7__ crackers.

Act it out to solve. Draw to show your work.

1. Min has 13 marbles.
   She gives some away.
   She has 5 left.
   How many marbles does
   she give away?

   Min gives away _____ marbles.

1. Cleo ate 12 cherries. Ben ate 7 cherries. How many fewer cherries did Ben eat than Cleo?

   ○ 8
   ○ 7
   ○ 6
   ○ 5

3. Dawn had some chalk. She gave away 5 pieces. Now she has 9 pieces of chalk. How many pieces of chalk did Dawn start with?

   ○ 14
   ○ 9
   ○ 6
   ○ 4

2. Josh picked 11 lemons. He used 4 lemons to make lemonade. How many lemons does Josh have now?

   ○ 15
   ○ 8
   ○ 7
   ○ 6

4. Mrs. Grasso picks 16 apples. She uses some apples in a pie. She has 9 left. How many apples did Mrs. Grasso use?

   ○ 6
   ○ 7
   ○ 8
   ○ 9

Choose a way to solve. Draw or write to explain.

5. Sue has 15 tomatoes. Her family eats some of them. Now Sue has 9 tomatoes. How many did her family eat?

_____ tomatoes

Name _____

Lesson 13

COMMON CORE STANDARD CC.1.OA.1

Lesson Objective: Solve addition and subtraction problem situations using the strategy *make a model*.

Problem Solving • Add or Subtract

There are 12 skunks in the woods.

Some skunks walk away.

There are 8 skunks still in the woods.

How many skunks walk away?

Unlock the Problem

What do I need to find?

how many
walk away   ~skunks~

What information do I need to use?

12 skunks in the woods

8 skunks still in the woods

Show how to solve the problem.

	8

12

4 walk away

8 skunks still in the woods

12 skunks

Make a model to solve.

Use ▢▢ to help you.

1. There are 15 frogs on a log.

   Some frogs hop away.

   There are 7 frogs still on the log.

   How many frogs hop away?

7	

15

_____ frogs hop away

Name _____

1. Mitchell finds 6 shells on the beach. Now he has 13 shells. How many shells did Mitchell start with?

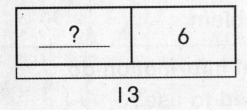

13

○ 1   ○ 12

○ 7   ○ 13

2. Elsa makes 18 cards. She gives some to her friends. Now she has 9 cards left. How many cards does Elsa give to her friends?

○ 27   ○ 10

○ 11   ○ 9

3. Mr. Stuart buys 11 erasers. He gives 7 of them away. How many erasers does he have left?

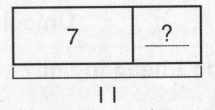

11

○ 3   ○ 7

○ 4   ○ 18

4. Flora has 8 pencils in her pencil case. Pat has 4 more pencils than Flora. How many pencils does Pat have?

○ 2   ○ 11

○ 4   ○ 12

5. Mr. Diaz gives music lessons to 12 children. 5 children are girls. How many children are boys?

_____ boys

Lesson 14

COMMON CORE STANDARD CC.1.OA.1

Lesson Objective: Choose an operation and strategy to solve an addition or subtraction word problem.

Name _____

Choose an Operation

Liz has 15 stuffed animals. She gives away 6. How many stuffed animals are left?

THINK
Liz gives some away.
So, I subtract.
Circle **subtract**.

add   (subtract)

$$15 \ominus 6 = 9$$

___9___ stuffed animals

Circle add or subtract.
Write a number sentence to solve.

1. Misha has 11 crackers.
   He eats 2 crackers.
   How many crackers are left?

   add   subtract

   _____ crackers   ___ ◯ ___ = ___

2. Lynn has 5 shells.
   Dan has 7 shells.
   How many shells do Lynn and Dan have?

   add   subtract

   _____ shells   ___ ◯ ___ = ___

1. Lisa bakes 6 muffins. Max bakes some more. They bake 14 muffins. Which number sentence shows how many muffins Max bakes?

   ○ $14 + 6 = 20$
   ○ $7 + 7 = 14$
   ○ $14 - 6 = 8$
   ○ $14 - 7 = 7$

2. Pat sees 6 dogs. Megan sees 4 more dogs than Pat. Which number sentence shows how many dogs they see?

   ○ $6 - 4 = 2$
   ○ $6 + 4 + 4 = 14$
   ○ $6 + 6 + 4 = 16$
   ○ $6 + 6 = 12$

3. Julia has a fish tank with 12 fish. 4 are clown fish. The rest are goldfish. Which number sentence shows how many goldfish are in the fish tank?

   ○ $12 - 4 = 8$
   ○ $10 + 2 = 12$
   ○ $4 + 2 = 6$
   ○ $16 - 12 = 4$

4. Jason and Lucy eat 13 raisins. Jason eats 8 raisins. Which number sentence shows how many raisins Lucy eats?

   ○ $13 + 8 = 21$
   ○ $9 + 4 = 13$
   ○ $5 + 5 = 10$
   ○ $13 - 8 = 5$

5. Jane makes 16 cupcakes. Some have chocolate frosting. 7 have strawberry frosting. How many cupcakes have chocolate frosting?

   _____

Name _____

Lesson 15

COMMON CORE STANDARD CC.1.OA.2

Lesson Objective: Solve adding to and putting together situations using the strategy *draw a picture*.

Problem Solving •
Use Addition Strategies

Tory has 9 toys. Bob has 4 toys.
Joy has 2 toys. How many toys
do they have?

Unlock the Problem

What do I need to find?	**What information do I need to use?**
how many **toys** they have	Tory has ___9___ toys. Bob has ___4___ toys. Joy has ___2___ toys.

Show how to solve the problem.

_____ $+$ _____ $+$ _____ $=$ _____   _____ toys

Draw a picture to solve.

1. Rick has 7 books.

   He gets 2 more books.

   He then gets 2 more books.

   How many books does

   Rick have now?   _____ books

1. Jim has 3 apples. Kay has 4 apples. Lee has 3 apples. How many apples do they have?

○ 10　　○ 8
○ 9　　○ 7

2. Jake has 2 pens. Penny has 0 pens. Ada has 7 pens. How many pens do they have?

○ 0　　○ 9
○ 5　　○ 10

3. Diego plays 6 math games. He plays 5 more math games. Then he plays 1 more math game. How many math games does Diego play?

○ 9　　○ 11
○ 10　　○ 12

4. There are 6 beads in a pouch. Trina adds 6 beads. Marcus adds 5 beads. How many beads are in the pouch now?

○ 11　　○ 15
○ 12　　○ 17

5. Draw a picture to solve.
Cindy puts 8 red marbles in a bag.
She puts 9 blue marbles in the bag.
Then she puts 2 green marbles in the bag.
How many marbles are in the bag now?

_____ marbles

Name _____

Lesson 16

COMMON CORE STANDARD CC.1.OA.3
Lesson Objective: Understand and apply the Additive Identity Property for Addition.

Algebra • Add Zero

Use ⚪ to show each number.
Add. Write the sum.

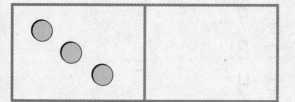

$3 + 0 = \underline{3}$

$0 + 2 = \underline{2}$

When you add zero to a number,
the sum is that number.

Use ⚪ to show each number.
Draw the ⚪. Write the sum.

1.

$0 + 4 = \underline{}$

2.

$6 + 0 = \underline{}$

3.

$0 + 1 = \underline{}$

4.

$0 + 5 = \underline{}$

1. What is the sum?

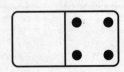

0 + 4 = _____

○ 4   ○ 3

○ 2   ○ 0

2. 7 frogs are in a pond. No frogs join them. How many frogs are there now?

○ 0
○ 3
○ 5
○ 7

3. Brad found 8 acorns. Siri did not find any acorns. How many acorns did they find?

○ 9
○ 8
○ 4
○ 0

4. What is the sum for 0 + 5?

○ 3
○ 4
○ 5
○ 6

PROBLEM SOLVING

Write the addition sentence to solve.

5. 6 turtles swim.
   No turtles join them.
   How many turtles are there now?

_____ + _____ = _____

_____ turtles

Name _____

Lesson 17

COMMON CORE STANDARD CC.1.OA.3
Lesson Objective: Explore the
Commutative Property of Addition.

Algebra • Add in Any Order

Write an addition sentence.
Change the order of the addends.
The sum is still the same.

Turn the cube
train around.

$5 + 3 = \underline{8}$
sum

$\underline{} + \underline{5} = \underline{8}$
sum

Use 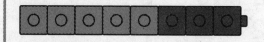 to add. Write
the sum.

**Change the order of the
addends. Color to match.
Write the addition sentence.**

1.

$1 + 5 = \underline{}$

$\underline{} + \underline{} = \underline{}$

2.

$3 + 1 = \underline{}$

$\underline{} + \underline{} = \underline{}$

Name _____

1. Which shows the same addends in a different order?

$$3 + 5 = 8$$

- ○ $3 + 4 = 7$
- ○ $3 + 5 = 8$
- ○ $5 + 4 = 9$
- ○ $5 + 3 = 8$

2. Which shows the same addends in a different order?

$$6 + 4 = \underline{\hspace{1cm}}$$

- ○ $6 + 6 = \underline{\hspace{1cm}}$
- ○ $6 + 4 = \underline{\hspace{1cm}}$
- ○ $4 + 6 = \underline{\hspace{1cm}}$
- ○ $4 + 5 = \underline{\hspace{1cm}}$

3. Which shows the same addends in a different order?

$$8 + 2 = 10$$

- ○ $2 + 6 = 8$
- ○ $2 + 8 = 10$
- ○ $8 + 1 = 9$
- ○ $8 + 2 = 10$

4. Look at the connecting cubes. Which addition fact **cannot** be shown with them?

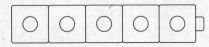

- ○ $5 + 2 = 7$
- ○ $2 + 3 = 5$
- ○ $3 + 2 = 5$
- ○ $0 + 5 = 5$

PROBLEM SOLVING  REAL WORLD

Draw pictures to match the addition sentences.
Write the sums.

5. $5 + 2 = \underline{\hspace{1cm}}$

$2 + 5 = \underline{\hspace{1cm}}$

Lesson 18

COMMON CORE STANDARD CC.1.OA.3

Lesson Objective: Understand and apply the Commutative Property of Addition for sums within 20.

Algebra · Add in Any Order

You can change the order of the addends.
The sum is the same.

$$\begin{array}{r} 5 \\ + 2 \\ \hline 7 \end{array}$$

$$\begin{array}{r} 2 \\ + 5 \\ \hline 7 \end{array}$$

Add. Change the order of the addends. Add again.

1.

$$\begin{array}{r} 3 \\ + 1 \\ \hline \end{array}$$

$$\begin{array}{r} \square \\ + \square \\ \hline \square \end{array}$$

2.

$$\begin{array}{r} 4 \\ + 2 \\ \hline \end{array}$$

$$\begin{array}{r} \square \\ + \square \\ \hline \square \end{array}$$

3.

$$\begin{array}{r} 8 \\ + 3 \\ \hline \end{array}$$

$$\begin{array}{r} \square \\ + \square \\ \hline \square \end{array}$$

4.

$$\begin{array}{r} 9 \\ + 5 \\ \hline \end{array}$$

$$\begin{array}{r} \square \\ + \square \\ \hline \square \end{array}$$

1. Which shows the same addends in a different order?

$$8 + 3 = 11$$

- ○ $8 + 2 = 10$
- ○ $3 + 8 = 11$
- ○ $7 + 4 = 11$
- ○ $3 + 9 = 12$

3. Which shows the same addends in a different order?

$$7 + 8 = 15$$

- ○ $8 + 5 = 13$
- ○ $7 + 7 = 14$
- ○ $9 + 6 = 15$
- ○ $8 + 7 = 15$

2. Which shows the same addends in a different order?

$$9 + 4 = 13$$

- ○ $4 + 9 = 13$
- ○ $5 + 8 = 13$
- ○ $4 + 8 = 12$
- ○ $8 + 3 = 11$

4. Which shows the same addends in a different order?

$$6 + 2 = 8$$

- ○ $6 + 4 = 10$
- ○ $3 + 6 = 9$
- ○ $2 + 6 = 8$
- ○ $5 + 2 = 7$

5. Add. Change the order of the addends.
Add again.

$$9 + 6 = \boxed{}$$

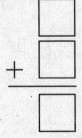

Name _____

Lesson 19

COMMON CORE STANDARD CC.1.OA.3
Lesson Objective: Use the Associative
Property of Addition to add three addends.

Algebra • Add 3 Numbers

You can add numbers in any order.

$3 + 4 + 1 = 8$

$3 + 4 + 1 = 8$

$\underline{7} + 1 = 8$

$3 + 4 + 1 = 8$

$3 + \underline{5} = 8$

**Use circles to change which two addends you add
first. Complete the addition sentences.**

1. $2 + 1 + 8 = 11$

$\underline{} + 8 = 11$

$2 + 1 + 8 = 11$

$2 + \underline{} = 11$

2. $7 + 2 + 3 = 12$

$\underline{} + 3 = 12$

$7 + 2 + 3 = 12$

$7 + \underline{} = 12$

1. What is the sum of
   4 + 1 + 5?

   ○ 5
   ○ 6
   ○ 9
   ○ 10

2. What is the sum of
   2 + 8 + 2?

   ○ 6
   ○ 8
   ○ 10
   ○ 12

3. What is the sum of
   5 + 0 + 3?

   ○ 8
   ○ 10
   ○ 12
   ○ 14

4. What is the sum of
   7 + 3 + 4?

   ○ 12
   ○ 13
   ○ 14
   ○ 15

PROBLEM SOLVING  REAL WORLD

5. Choose three numbers from 1 to 6.
   Write the numbers in an addition sentence.
   Show two ways to find the sum.

Name _____

Lesson 20

COMMON CORE STANDARD CC.1.OA.3

Lesson Objective: Understand and apply
the Associative Property or Commutative
Property of Addition to add three addends.

Algebra • Add 3 Numbers

What strategies help you add 3 numbers?

$$\begin{array}{r} 4 \\ 4 \\ + 6 \\ \hline 14 \end{array}$$

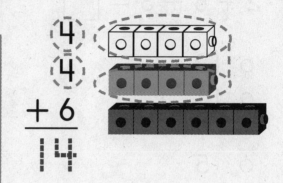

$$\begin{array}{r} 4 \\ 4 \\ + 6 \\ \hline 14 \end{array}$$

$4 + 6$ make a 10.

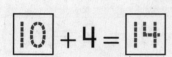

$$\boxed{10} + 4 = \boxed{14}$$

$4 + 4 = 8$ is
a doubles fact.

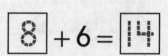

$$\boxed{8} + 6 = \boxed{14}$$

**Choose a strategy. Circle two addends
to add first. Write the sum.
Then find the total sum.**

1.
$$\begin{array}{r} 7 \\ 3 \\ + 3 \\ \hline 13 \end{array} \qquad \boxed{10}$$

2.
$$\begin{array}{r} 2 \\ 2 \\ + 8 \\ \hline \end{array} \qquad \Box$$

3.
$$\begin{array}{r} 4 \\ 3 \\ + 3 \\ \hline \end{array} \qquad \Box$$

4.
$$\begin{array}{r} 5 \\ 5 \\ + 4 \\ \hline \end{array} \qquad \Box$$

1. What is the sum?

$$2 + 6 + 3 = \square$$

○ 13
○ 11
○ 9
○ 5

3. What is the sum?

$$4 + 8 + 4 = \square$$

○ 10
○ 12
○ 14
○ 16

2. What is the sum?

$$6 + 5 + 4 = \square$$

○ 15
○ 11
○ 10
○ 9

4. What is the sum?

$$7 + 1 + 2 = \square$$

○ 8
○ 9
○ 10
○ 12

PROBLEM SOLVING REAL WORLD

Draw a picture. Write the number sentence.

5. Don has 4 black dogs.
Tim has 3 small dogs.
Sue has 3 big dogs.
How many dogs do they have?

____ + ____ + ____ = ____ dogs

Name _____

Think Addition to Subtract

What is 7 − 4?

(Think)   4 + __3__ = 7   

(So)   7 − 4 = __3__   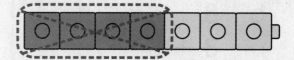

Use 🎲🎲 **to model the number sentences.**
Draw 🎲🎲 **to show your work.**

1. What is 11 − 2?

(Think)   2 + ___ = 11

(So)   11 − 2 = ___

2. What is 10 − 6?

(Think)   6 + ___ = 10

(So)   10 − 6 = ___

3. What is 6 − 1?

(Think)   1 + ___ = 6

(So)   6 − 1 = ___

1. Which addition sentence can you use to help you subtract $14 - 8$?

   ○ $4 + 4 = 8$
   ○ $8 + 6 = 14$
   ○ $8 + 8 = 16$
   ○ $14 + 8 = 22$

3. Which subtraction sentence can you solve by using $7 + 9 = 16$?

   ○ $9 - 7 = 2$
   ○ $10 - 6 = 4$
   ○ $16 - 9 = 7$
   ○ $16 - 8 = 8$

2. Which addition fact helps solve the subtraction fact $12 - 5$?

   ○ $7 + 5 = 12$
   ○ $12 + 5 = 17$
   ○ $5 + 8 = 13$
   ○ $6 + 5 = 11$

4. Which addition fact helps solve the subtraction fact $13 - 4$?

   ○ $8 + 6 = 14$
   ○ $8 + 5 = 13$
   ○ $9 + 3 = 12$
   ○ $9 + 4 = 13$

PROBLEM SOLVING  REAL WORLD

5. Write a number sentence to solve.
   I have 18 pieces of fruit.
   9 are apples.
   The rest are oranges.
   How many are oranges?

   _____ oranges

Lesson 22

COMMON CORE STANDARD CC.1.OA.4
Lesson Objective: Use addition as a strategy to subtract numbers within 20.

Use Think Addition to Subtract

Think of an addition fact to help you subtract.	Think	
	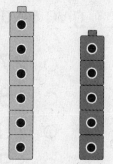	
$11 - 6 = \underline{\ ?\ }$	$6 + \underline{\ 5\ } = 11$	$11 - 6 = \underline{\ 5\ }$

Use an addition fact to help you subtract.

1. What is $9 - 4$?

Use $\quad 4 + \underline{\quad} = 9$

So $\quad 9 - 4 = \underline{\quad}$

2. What is $10 - 6$?

Use $\quad 6 + \underline{\quad} = 10$

So $\quad 10 - 6 = \underline{\quad}$

3. What is $12 - 5$?

Use $\quad 5 + \underline{\quad} = 12$

So $\quad 12 - 5 = \underline{\quad}$

4. What is $8 - 5$?

Use $\quad 5 + \underline{\quad} = 8$

So $\quad 8 - 5 = \underline{\quad}$

1. Which addition fact can you use to help you subtract $11 - 6$?

   ○ $6 + 1 = 7$
   ○ $10 + 1 = 11$
   ○ $5 + 6 = 11$
   ○ $11 + 6 = 17$

2. What number is missing?

$$\begin{array}{r} 6 \\ + 8 \\ \hline 14 \end{array} \qquad \begin{array}{r} 14 \\ - 8 \\ \hline \square \end{array}$$

   ○ 6
   ○ 8
   ○ 10
   ○ 14

3. Maria has 18 pears. She gives some of them away. She has 9 pears left. How many pears does Maria give away?

   ○ 27
   ○ 18
   ○ 10
   ○ 9

4. Which subtraction sentence can you solve by using $9 + 6 = 15$?

   ○ $15 - 6 =$ _____
   ○ $15 - 7 =$ _____
   ○ $9 - 6 =$ _____
   ○ $16 - 9 =$ _____

PROBLEM SOLVING

5. Solve. Draw or write to show your work.

   I have 15 nickels.

   Some are old. 6 are new.

   How many nickels are old?

   _____ nickels

Name _____

Lesson 23

COMMON CORE STANDARD CC.1.OA.5

Lesson Objective: Use count on 1, 2, or 3 as a strategy to find sums within 20.

Count On

You can count on to find $4 + 3$.
Start with the greater addend.
Then count on. Write the sum.

To add 3,
count on 3.

◯   ◯   ◯

4   5   6   7

$4 + 3 = 7$

Circle the greater addend. Count on 1, 2, or 3.
Write the missing numbers.

1. $1 + 6$

◯   ◯

6   __

$1 + 6 = $ ___

2. $9 + 1$

◯   ◯

9   __

$9 + 1 = $ ___

3. $4 + 2$

◯   ◯   ◯

4   __   __

$4 + 2 = $ ___

4. $3 + 8$

◯   ◯   ◯   ◯

8   __   __   __

$3 + 8 = $ ___

1. What is the sum?

_____ = 5 + 2

○ 10　　○ 8

○ 9　　○ 7

3. What is the sum?

_____ = 8 + 1

○ 10　　○ 8

○ 9　　○ 7

2. What is the sum?

9
+ 3

○ 6　　○ 14

○ 12　　○ 16

4. What is the sum?

7
+ 3

○ 5　　○ 9

○ 7　　○ 10

5. Circle the greater addend.
Count on to find the sum.

8
+ 3

Name _____

Lesson 24

COMMON CORE STANDARD CC.1.OA.5
Lesson Objective: Use count back
1, 2, or 3 as a strategy to subtract.

Count Back

Count back to subtract.

Use 9 . Count back 3.
This shows counting back 3 from 9.

$6 \quad 7 \quad 8 \quad 9$

$9 - 3 = \underline{6}$

Use . Count back 1, 2, or 3.

Write the difference.

1. $5 - 1 = \underline{}$

$\underline{} \quad 5$

2. $7 - 2 = \underline{}$

$\underline{} \quad \underline{} \quad 7$

3. $6 - 3 = \underline{}$

$\underline{} \quad \underline{} \quad \underline{} \quad 6$

1. Count back. What is the difference?

$$10 - 2 = \boxed{}$$

- ○ 8
- ○ 9
- ○ 10
- ○ 12

2. Count back. What is the difference?

$$9 - 3 = \boxed{}$$

- ○ 5
- ○ 6
- ○ 7
- ○ 8

3. Luis had 11 markers. He gave 2 markers to Elena. How many markers does Luis have now?

- ○ 13
- ○ 10
- ○ 9
- ○ 8

4. Vicky made 8 muffins. Her family ate some. Now there are 5 muffins. How many muffins did her family eat? Which subtraction sentence answers the problem?

- ○ $5 - 3 = 2$
- ○ $10 - 5 = 5$
- ○ $8 - 3 = 5$
- ○ $8 - 2 = 6$

PROBLEM SOLVING

Write a subtraction sentence to solve.

5. Tina has 12 pencils.
   She gives away 3 pencils.
   How many pencils are left?

   _____ − _____ = _____

   _____ pencils

Lesson 25

COMMON CORE STANDARD CC.1.OA.6
Lesson Objective: Build fluency for addition within 10.

Addition to 10

You can use ☐ to help you add.

```
  4  ☐☐☐☐
+ 2  ☐☐
─────
  6
```

```
  6  ☐☐☐☐☐☐
+ 3  ☐☐☐
─────
```

Use ☐. Write the sum.

1.
```
  1  ☐
+ 2  ☐☐
─────
```

2.
```
  4  ☐☐☐☐
+ 1  ☐
─────
```

3.
```
  3  ☐☐☐
+ 5  ☐☐☐☐☐
─────
```

4.
```
  2  ☐☐
+ 3  ☐☐☐
─────
```

1. What is the sum?

$$\begin{array}{r} 3 \\ +\ 7 \\ \hline \end{array}$$

- ○ 8
- ○ 9
- ○ 10
- ○ 11

3. What is the sum?

$$\begin{array}{r} 5 \\ +\ 4 \\ \hline \end{array}$$

- ○ 3
- ○ 8
- ○ 9
- ○ 10

2. What is the sum?

$$\begin{array}{r} 4 \\ +\ 4 \\ \hline \end{array}$$

- ○ 4
- ○ 6
- ○ 7
- ○ 8

4. What is the sum?

$$\begin{array}{r} 0 \\ +\ 1 \\ \hline \end{array}$$

- ○ 0
- ○ 1
- ○ 2
- ○ 10

PROBLEM SOLVING REAL WORLD

Add. Write the sum. Use the sum and the key to color the flowers.

5.

$$\begin{array}{r} 2 \\ +\ 5 \\ \hline \end{array}$$

4 + 5 = ____

$$\begin{array}{r} 7 \\ +\ 1 \\ \hline \end{array}$$

KEY

6	YELLOW
7	RED
8	PURPLE
9	PINK

Subtraction from 10 or Less

You can use  to help you subtract.

$$6$$
$$- \ 3$$
$$3$$

$$3$$
$$- \ 1$$
$$2$$

Write the subtraction problem.

1.

$$7$$
$$- \ 4$$

2.

$$5$$
$$- \ 3$$

3.

$$8$$
$$- \ 1$$

4.

$$4$$
$$- \ 2$$

Core Standards for Math, Grade 1

1. What is the difference?

$$\begin{array}{r} 6 \\ -5 \\ \hline \end{array}$$

○ 4
○ 3
○ 2
○ 1

2. What is the difference?

$$\begin{array}{r} 10 \\ -7 \\ \hline \end{array}$$

○ 4
○ 3
○ 2
○ 0

PROBLEM SOLVING

Solve.

3. 6 birds are in the tree.
None of the birds fly away.
How many birds are left?

_____ – _____ = _____

Lesson 27

COMMON CORE STANDARD CC.1.OA.6

Lesson Objective: Use doubles as a strategy to solve addition facts with sums within 20.

Add Doubles

The addends are the same in a doubles fact.

$$\underline{3} + \underline{3} = 6$$

Draw to show the addends.
Write the missing numbers.

1.
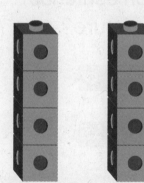

$$\underline{\quad} + \underline{\quad} = 8$$

2.
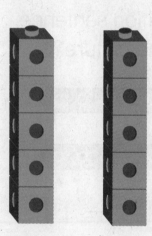

$$\underline{\quad} + \underline{\quad} = 10$$

3.

$$\underline{\quad} + \underline{\quad} = 4$$

4.

$$\underline{\quad} + \underline{\quad} = 2$$

Core Standards for Math, Grade 1

1. Which addition sentence matches the picture?

○ 3 + 3 = 6
○ 4 + 4 = 8
○ 5 + 5 = 10
○ 6 + 6 = 12

3. Which addition sentence matches the picture?

○ 4 + 4 = 8
○ 3 + 3 = 6
○ 2 + 2 = 4
○ 1 + 1 = 2

2. Which addition sentence matches the picture?

○ 7 + 7 = 14
○ 8 + 8 = 16
○ 9 + 9 = 18
○ 10 + 10 = 20

4. Which addition sentence matches the picture?

○ 6 + 6 = 12
○ 7 + 7 = 14
○ 8 + 8 = 16
○ 9 + 9 = 18

5. Write the doubles fact that matches the picture.

____ + ____ = ____

Core Standards for Math, Grade 1

Name _____

Lesson 28
COMMON CORE STANDARD CC.1.OA.6
Lesson Objective: Use doubles to create
equivalent but easier sums.

Use Doubles to Add

Use a doubles fact to solve $4 + 3$.
Break apart 4 into $1 + 3$.

○ ● ● ● ● ● ●

1　　+　　3　　+　　3

1　　+　　　　6　　　=　7

THINK
$3 + 3 = 6$.
1 more than 6 is 7.

So, $4 + 3 = \underline{7}$.

Use ○ ● to model. Break apart
to make a doubles fact. Add.

1. $6 + 5$

○ ● ● ● ● ● ● ● ● ● ●

$\underline{1}$　+　___　+　___

___　+　___　=　___

So, $6 + 5 = $ ___.

2. $8 + 7$

○ ● ● ● ● ● ● ● ● ● ● ● ● ● ●

___　+　___　+　___

___　+　___　=　___

So, $8 + 7 = $ ___.

Core Standards for Math, Grade 1

1. Which has the same sum as 7 + 6?

   ○ 1 + 7 + 7
   ○ 1 + 6 + 6
   ○ 4 + 4 + 2
   ○ 3 + 3 + 3

2. Which has the same sum as 4 + 3?

   ○ 7 + 7 + 1
   ○ 5 + 5 + 1
   ○ 4 + 4 + 1
   ○ 1 + 3 + 3

3. Which has the same sum as 7 + 8?

   ○ 3 + 3 + 1
   ○ 4 + 4 + 1
   ○ 7 + 7 + 1
   ○ 8 + 8 + 2

4. Which has the same sum as 5 + 6?

   ○ 5 + 1 + 6
   ○ 5 + 5 + 1
   ○ 6 + 5 + 5
   ○ 6 + 6 + 5

PROBLEM SOLVING

Solve. Draw or write to explain.

5. Bo has 6 toys. Mia has 7 toys. How many toys do they have?

   _____ toys

Core Standards for Math, Grade 1

COMMON CORE STANDARD CC.1.OA.6
Lesson Objective: Use doubles plus 1 and doubles minus 1 as strategies to find sums within 20.

Doubles Plus 1 and Doubles Minus 1

You can use doubles plus one facts and doubles minus one to add.

Use doubles fact 3 + 3 = 6.

doubles plus one

doubles minus one

$$3 + 4 = 7$$

$$3 + 2 = 5$$

Use doubles plus one or doubles minus one to add.

1.

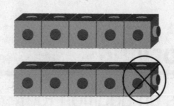

$$5 + 6 = \underline{\hspace{1cm}}$$

$$5 + 4 = \underline{\hspace{1cm}}$$

2.

$$2 + 3 = \underline{\hspace{1cm}}$$

$$2 + 1 = \underline{\hspace{1cm}}$$

1. Which doubles fact helps you solve $3 + 4 = 7$?

    ○ $4 + 4 = 8$
    ○ $5 + 5 = 10$
    ○ $6 + 6 = 12$
    ○ $7 + 7 = 14$

3. Which doubles fact helps you solve $7 + 6 = 13$?

    ○ $5 + 5 = 10$
    ○ $6 + 6 = 12$
    ○ $8 + 8 = 16$
    ○ $9 + 9 = 18$

2. Which doubles fact helps you solve $5 + 4 = 9$?

    ○ $3 + 3 = 6$
    ○ $4 + 4 = 8$
    ○ $6 + 6 = 12$
    ○ $7 + 7 = 14$

4. Which doubles fact helps you solve $8 + 9 = 17$?

    ○ $5 + 5 = 10$
    ○ $6 + 6 = 12$
    ○ $7 + 7 = 14$
    ○ $9 + 9 = 18$

PROBLEM SOLVING  REAL WORLD

5. Andy writes an addition fact. One addend is 9. The sum is 17. What is the other addend? Write the addition fact.

    _____ + _____ = 17

Lesson 30

COMMON CORE STANDARD CC.1.OA.6

Lesson Objective: Use the strategies count on, doubles, doubles plus 1, and doubles minus 1 to practice addition facts within 20.

Practice the Strategies

You can use different addition strategies to find sums.

Count On	Doubles
 $6 + 2 = 8$	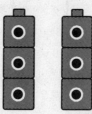 $3 + 3 = 6$

Doubles Plus 1	Doubles Minus 1
 $5 + 6 = 11$	 $5 + 4 = 9$

1. Count on 1.

$7 + 1 =$ ___

2. Count on 2.

$7 + 2 =$ ___

3. Count on 3.

$7 + 3 =$ ___

4. Use doubles.

$6 + 6 =$ ___

5. Use doubles plus 1.

$6 + 7 =$ ___

6. Use doubles minus 1.

$6 + 5 =$ ___

1. What is the missing sum?

Doubles
3 + 3 = 6
4 + 4 = 8
5 + 5 = 10
6 + 6 = _____

○ 12
○ 14
○ 16
○ 18

3. What is the missing sum?

Count On 3
3 + 3 = 6
4 + 3 = 7
5 + 3 = 8
6 + 3 = _____

○ 6
○ 7
○ 8
○ 9

2. What is the missing sum?

Doubles Plus One
6 + 7 = 13
7 + 8 = 15
8 + 9 = _____

○ 15
○ 16
○ 17
○ 18

4. What is the missing sum?

Doubles Minus One
3 + 2 = 5
4 + 3 = 7
5 + 4 = _____

○ 8
○ 9
○ 10
○ 11

5. What is the sum?

8 + 3 = _____

Lesson 31

COMMON CORE STANDARD CC.1.OA.6
Lesson Objective: Use a ten frame to add 10 and an addend less than 10.

Add 10 and More

You can use counters and a ten frame to add a number to 10.

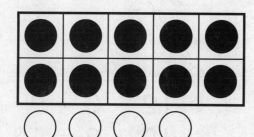

Find 10 + 4.

$$\begin{array}{r} 10 \\ + \ 4 \\ \hline 14 \end{array}$$

Draw ◯. **Show the number that is added to 10.**
Write the sum.

1.

$$\begin{array}{r} 10 \\ + \ 3 \\ \hline \end{array}$$

2.

$$\begin{array}{r} 10 \\ + \ 7 \\ \hline \end{array}$$

1. What number sentence does this model show?

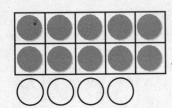

○ $10 - 4 = 6$
○ $5 + 4 = 9$
○ $7 + 6 = 13$
○ $10 + 4 = 14$

3. What number sentence does this model show?

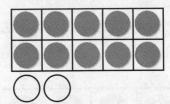

○ $5 + 2 = 7$
○ $12 - 3 = 9$
○ $10 + 2 = 12$
○ $10 + 3 = 13$

2. What number sentence does this model show?

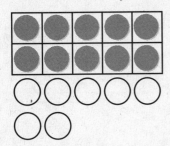

○ $10 + 7 = 17$
○ $10 + 5 = 15$
○ $5 + 2 = 7$
○ $10 - 7 = 3$

4. What number sentence does this model show?

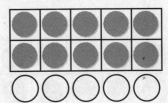

○ $5 + 5 = 10$
○ $10 - 5 = 5$
○ $10 + 5 = 15$
○ $10 + 10 = 20$

5. Draw ● to show 10.
Draw ○ to show the other addend. Write the sum.

$$\begin{array}{r} 10 \\ + \ 6 \\ \hline \end{array}$$

Lesson 32

COMMON CORE STANDARD CC.1.OA.6

Lesson Objective: Use make a ten as a strategy to find sums within 20.

Make a 10 to Add

Show 8 + 5 with counters and a ten frame.

Use ⃝.

8

5

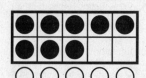

Make a ten. Add.

$$10$$
$$+\ 3$$
$$\overline{13}$$

So, $8 + 5 =$ ___13___.

Draw ⃝ to show the second addend. Make a ten. Add.

1. $8 + 6$

8

6

$$10$$
$$+\ 4$$

So, $8 + 6 =$ ____.

2. $9 + 7$

9

7

$$10$$
$$+\ 6$$

So, $9 + 7 =$ ____.

Core Standards for Math, Grade 1

1. What number sentence does this model show?

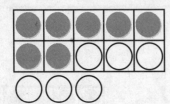

- ○ $7 - 3 = 4$
- ○ $7 + 6 = 13$
- ○ $10 + 3 = 13$
- ○ $10 + 7 = 17$

3. What number sentence does this model show?

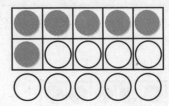

- ○ $9 - 5 = 4$
- ○ $15 - 5 = 10$
- ○ $6 + 9 = 15$
- ○ $6 + 10 = 16$

2. What number sentence does this model show?

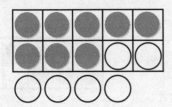

- ○ $7 + 7 = 14$
- ○ $14 - 4 = 10$
- ○ $8 + 4 = 12$
- ○ $8 + 6 = 14$

4. What number sentence does this model show?

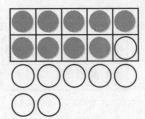

- ○ $9 + 8 = 17$
- ○ $9 + 7 = 16$
- ○ $9 + 5 = 14$
- ○ $17 - 7 = 10$

PROBLEM SOLVING

Solve.

5. $10 + 6$ has the same sum as $7 +$ _____.

Name _____

Lesson 33

COMMON CORE STANDARD CC.1.OA.6

Lesson Objective: Use numbers to show how to use the make a ten strategy to add.

Use Make a 10 to Add

What is 9 + 5? Make a 10 to add.

Use ◯ and a ten frame.
Show the addends.

Make a 10.
Add.

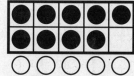

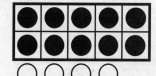

So, 9 + 5 = __14__.

Show the greater addend in the ten frame.

Draw ◯. Make a ten to add.

1. 8 + 5

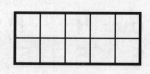

$\begin{array}{r} 10 \\ +\ 3 \\ \hline \end{array}$

So, 8 + 5 = ____.

2. 7 + 4

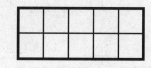

$\begin{array}{r} 10 \\ +\ 1 \\ \hline \end{array}$

So, 7 + 4 = ____.

1. Which shows a way to make a ten to solve 9 + 3?

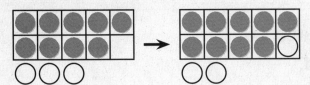

- ○ 9 + 1 + 3
- ○ 9 + 1 + 2
- ○ 5 + 5 + 3
- ○ 3 + 7 + 3

3. Which shows a way to make a ten to solve 8 + 4?

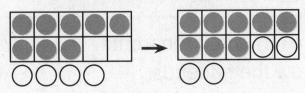

- ○ 5 + 3 + 2
- ○ 5 + 5 + 4
- ○ 8 + 1 + 2
- ○ 8 + 2 + 2

2. Which shows a way to make a ten to solve 9 + 6?

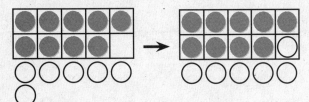

- ○ 5 + 4 + 5
- ○ 6 + 6 + 4
- ○ 9 + 1 + 5
- ○ 5 + 5 + 6

4. Which shows a way to make a ten to solve 6 + 5?

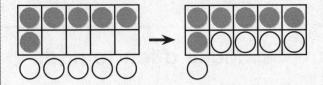

- ○ 6 + 4 + 1
- ○ 6 + 4 + 4
- ○ 5 + 5 + 5
- ○ 5 + 4 + 1

5. Write to show how you make a ten. Then add.
What is 9 + 7?

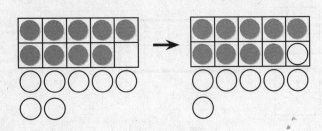

_____ + _____ + _____

_____ + _____ = _____

So, 9 + 7 = _____

Name _____

Lesson 34

COMMON CORE STANDARD CC.1.OA.6
Lesson Objective: Use make a 10 as a
strategy to subtract.

Use 10 to Subtract

Find 14 − 9.

Start with 9 cubes.

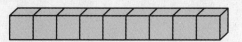

Make a 10.

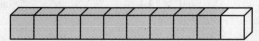

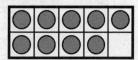

Add cubes to make 14.

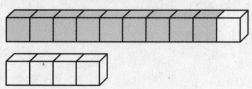

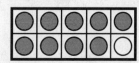

Count what you added.

You added __5__.

So, 14 − 9 = __5__.

Use 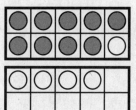. Make a ten to subtract.
Draw to show your work.

1. 12 − 8 = __?__   2. 15 − 9 = __?__

   12 − 8 = ___   15 − 9 = ___

1. Use ten frames to make a ten to help you subtract.

$15 - 9 =$ ___?___

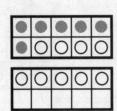

7 ○   6 ○   5 ○   4 ○

2. Use ten frames to make a ten to help you subtract. Angel has 16 grapes. He eats some of them. He has 7 grapes left. How many grapes did Angel eat?

9 ○   8 ○   7 ○   6 ○

3. Mr. Dunn had 12 eggs. He used 8 eggs for breakfast. How many eggs are left?

20 ○   6 ○   4 ○   2 ○

4. Write the number sentence that matches the subtraction shown in the ten frames.

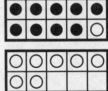

_____ – _____ = _____

Name _____

Lesson 35

COMMON CORE STANDARD CC.1.OA.6
Lesson Objective: Subtract by breaking apart to make a ten.

Break Apart to Subtract

What is 14 − 5?

Start with 14. Make a ten.

Take __4__ from 14.

$$\underline{14} − \underline{4} = \underline{10}$$

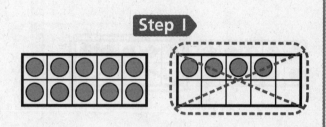

Step 1

Then take __1__ more.

$$\underline{10} − \underline{1} = \underline{9}$$

Step 2

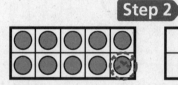

So, 14 − 5 = __9__

Subtract.

1. What is 17 − 9?

Take 7 counters from 17.

17 − 7 = ____

Step 1

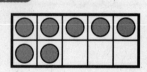

Then take ____ counters from 10.

____ − ____ = ____

Step 2

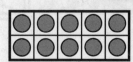 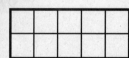

So, 17 − 9 = ____

1. Ray uses ten frames to find 15 − 7. Which is the correct answer?

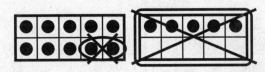

  ○ 5   ○ 7
  ○ 6   ○ 8

3. Rosa uses ten frames to find 16 − 9. How many will she subtract first from 16 to get to 10?

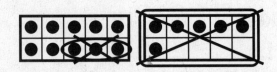

  ○ 6   ○ 8
  ○ 7   ○ 9

2. Make a ten to solve. What is 13 − 5?

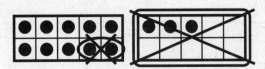

  ○ 3   ○ 8
  ○ 5   ○ 9

4. Make a ten to solve. What is 14 − 7?

  ○ 4   ○ 7
  ○ 6   ○ 8

5. There are 13 birds in the tree. 8 birds fly away. How many birds are still in the tree?

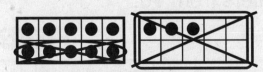

_____ − _____ = _____

_____ birds

Core Standards for Math, Grade 1

Lesson 36

COMMON CORE STANDARD CC.1.OA.6
Lesson Objective: Record related facts within 20.

Record Related Facts

Use the numbers to write four related facts.

$6 + 4 = 10$ $10 - 4 = 6$

THINK
Each number is in all four facts.

$4 + 6 = 10$ $10 - 6 = 4$

Use the numbers to make related facts.

1.

$6 + 8 = 14$ $\square - 8 = 6$

$8 + \square = 14$ $14 - 6 = \square$

2.

$\square + 7 = 9$ $9 - \square = 2$

$7 + 2 = 9$ $\square - 2 = 7$

3.

$5 + \square = 11$ $\square - 6 = 5$

$6 + 5 = 11$ $11 - \square = 6$

4.

$3 + 9 = 12$ $\square - 9 = 3$

$\square + 3 = 12$ $12 - \square = 9$

---

1. What is the missing number?

$$\square + 3 = 11$$

$$11 - 3 = \square$$

$$3 + \square = 11$$

$$11 - \square = 3$$

- ○ 3 ○ 9
- ○ 8 ○ 15

3. Which fact is a related fact?

$$8 + 7 = 15$$

$$15 - 7 = 8$$

- ○ $15 - 8 = 7$
- ○ $8 - 6 = 2$
- ○ $7 + 7 = 14$
- ○ $8 + 4 = 12$

2. What is the missing number?

$$\square + 4 = 12$$

$$12 - 4 = \square$$

$$4 + \square = 12$$

$$12 - \square = 4$$

- ○ 6 ○ 10
- ○ 8 ○ 13

4. Which fact is a related fact?

$$5 + 6 = 11$$

$$11 - 6 = 5$$

- ○ $5 + 8 = 13$
- ○ $6 - 5 = 1$
- ○ $6 + 6 = 12$
- ○ $11 - 5 = 6$

5. Write the missing related fact.

$$9 + 6 = 15 \qquad 15 - 9 = 6$$

$$6 + 9 = 15 \qquad \underline{\hspace{3cm}}$$

Lesson 37

COMMON CORE STANDARD CC.1.OA.6
Lesson Objective: Identify related addition
and subtraction facts within 20.

Identify Related Facts

If you know an addition fact, you will
also know the related subtraction fact.

Both facts use
2, 4, and 6.
They are related
facts.

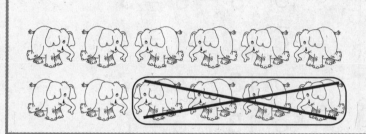

$$2 \oplus 4 \ominus 6$$

$$6 \ominus 4 \ominus 2$$

Add and subtract the related facts.

1.

$7 + 8 = \underline{\hspace{2em}}$

$15 - 8 = \underline{\hspace{2em}}$

2.

$7 + 4 = \underline{\hspace{2em}}$

$11 - 4 = \underline{\hspace{2em}}$

3.

$1 + 8 = \underline{\hspace{2em}}$

$9 - 8 = \underline{\hspace{2em}}$

Core Standards for Math, Grade 1

Name _____

1. Look at the pairs of facts. Which shows related facts?

$6 + 5 = 11$ $6 - 1 = 5$
$5 + 1 = 6$ $5 + 1 = 6$
   ○   ○

$6 + 5 = 11$ $16 - 8 = 8$
$5 + 5 = 10$ $5 + 9 = 14$
   ○   ○

3. Which subtraction fact is related to $8 + 5 = 13$?

○ $8 - 5 = 3$
○ $13 - 4 = 9$
○ $13 - 6 = 7$
○ $13 - 5 = 8$

2. Look at the pairs of facts. Which shows related facts?

$7 + 7 = 14$ $7 + 8 = 15$
$8 + 8 = 16$ $8 + 9 = 17$
   ○   ○

$7 + 7 = 14$ $1 + 7 = 8$
$14 - 7 = 7$ $17 - 8 = 9$
   ○   ○

4. Which addition fact is related to $10 - 7 = 3$?

○ $3 + 7 = 10$
○ $3 + 5 = 8$
○ $7 + 7 = 14$
○ $10 + 3 = 13$

5. Look at the addition fact.

$8 + 8 = 16$

Write a related subtraction fact.

_____

Lesson 38

COMMON CORE STANDARD CC.1.0A.6
Lesson Objective: Apply the inverse
relationship of addition and subtraction.

Use Addition to Check Subtraction

You can use addition to check subtraction.

You start with 8.
Take apart to subtract.

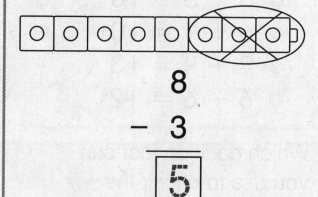

$$8$$
$$- 3$$
$$\overline{5}$$

THINK
Put the 5 and
3 back together.

Add to check.
You end with 8.

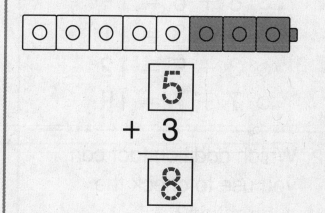

$$5$$
$$+ 3$$
$$\overline{8}$$

Use 🎲🎲 to help you. Subtract.
Then add to check your answer.

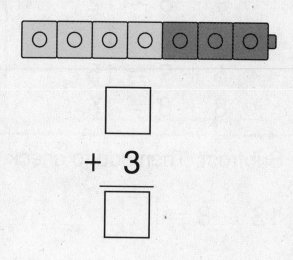

$$7$$
$$- 3$$
$$\overline{\square}$$

$$\square$$
$$+ 3$$
$$\overline{\square}$$

1. Which addition fact can you use to check the subtraction?

$$14 - 6 = \boxed{}$$

- ○ $8 + 6 = 14$
- ○ $8 + 3 = 11$
- ○ $3 + 9 = 12$
- ○ $7 + 7 = 14$

3. Which addition fact can you use to check the subtraction?

$$10 - 4 = 6$$

- ○ $8 + 8 = 16$
- ○ $6 + 4 = 10$
- ○ $9 + 4 = 13$
- ○ $6 + 6 = 12$

2. Which addition fact can you use to check the subtraction?

$$16 - 8 = \boxed{}$$

- ○ $4 + 8 = 12$
- ○ $3 + 8 = 11$
- ○ $6 + 9 = 15$
- ○ $8 + 8 = 16$

4. Which addition fact can you use to check the subtraction?

$$12 - 9 = 3$$

- ○ $3 + 3 = 6$
- ○ $3 + 9 = 12$
- ○ $9 + 9 = 18$
- ○ $3 + 6 = 9$

5. Subtract. Then add to check your answer.

$$13 - 8 = \boxed{}$$

$$\underline{} + \underline{} = \boxed{}$$

COMMON CORE STANDARD CC.1.OA.6

Lesson Objective: Represent equivalent forms of numbers using sums and differences within 20.

Algebra • Ways to Make Numbers to 20

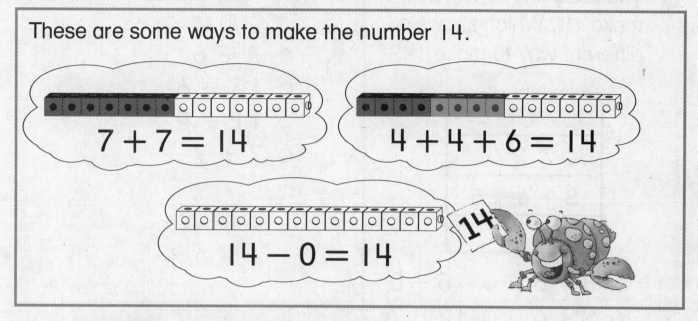

These are some ways to make the number 14.

$7 + 7 = 14$

$4 + 4 + 6 = 14$

$14 - 0 = 14$

Use 🎲 🎲 🎲 to show each way.

Cross out the way that does not make the number.

1. **7**	$8 - 1$	$3 + 4$	~~$2 + 3 + 1$~~
2. **15**	$7 + 6$	$15 - 0$	$8 + 7$
3. **13**	$4 + 4 + 5$	$9 - 4$	$6 + 7$
4. **9**	$8 + 2$	$3 + 3 + 3$	$10 - 1$
5. **18**	$9 + 9$	$9 - 9$	$18 - 0$

Name _____

1. The table shows ways to make 14. Which shows a different way to make 14?

14
7 + 7
3 + 6 + 5

○ 8 + 6   ○ 15 − 0
○ 9 + 6   ○ 12 − 7

2. The table shows ways to make 18. Which shows a different way to make 18?

18
9 + 9
4 + 6 + 8

○ 10 + 5   ○ 19 − 3
○ 15 + 1   ○ 10 + 8

3. Which way makes 13?

○ 7 + 6
○ 15 − 6
○ 11 − 2
○ 7 + 7

4. Which way makes 15?

○ 6 + 7 + 3
○ 10 − 5
○ 8 + 5
○ 7 + 3 + 5

5. Write two ways to make 12.

_____   _____

Lesson 40

COMMON CORE STANDARD CC.1.OA.6
Lesson Objective: Add and subtract
facts within 20 and demonstrate fluency for
addition and subtraction within 10.

Basic Facts to 20

Mr. Chi has 12 books.
He sells 3 books.
How many books are left?
What is 12 − 3?

> **THINK**
> I can count back.

> **THINK**
> I can use a related fact.

Start at 12.

Count 11, 10, _9_.

$3 + 9 = 12$

$12 - 3 =$ _9_

So, $12 - 3 =$ _9_.

Add or subtract.

1. $14 - 5 =$ ___	2. $9 + 2 =$ ___	3. $6 + 4 =$ ___
4. $12 - 6 =$ ___	5. $8 - 3 =$ ___	6. $7 + 5 =$ ___
7. $9 + 6 =$ ___	8. $13 - 9 =$ ___	9. $8 + 8 =$ ___

1. There are 13 frogs in a pond. Then 8 frogs hop away. How many frogs are still in the pond?

   ○ 5
   ○ 6
   ○ 7
   ○ 8

3. What is 14 − 5?

   ○ 7
   ○ 8
   ○ 9
   ○ 10

2. There are 8 cows at the farm. Then 4 cows come. How many cows are there now?

   ○ 9
   ○ 10
   ○ 11
   ○ 12

4. What is 8 + 6?

   ○ 12
   ○ 13
   ○ 14
   ○ 15

PROBLEM SOLVING  REAL WORLD

Solve. Draw or write to explain.

5. Kara has 9 drawings.
   She gives 4 away. How many drawings does Kara have now?

   _____ drawings

Lesson 41

COMMON CORE STANDARD CC.1.OA.6
Lesson Objective: Add and subtract within 20.

Add and Subtract within 20

You can use strategies to add or subtract.

- count on
- doubles
- doubles plus one
- count back
- related facts
- doubles minus one

What is $5 + 6$?

I can use doubles plus one.

$5 + 5 = 10$

So, $5 + 6 = \underline{11}$.

What is $12 - 4$?

I can use a related fact.

$8 + 4 = 12$

So, $12 - 4 = \underline{8}$.

Add or subtract.

1. $12 - 3 = $ _____

2. $8 + 9 = $ _____

3. $10 - 5 = $ _____

4. $13 - 7 = $ _____

5. $7 + 8 = $ _____

6. $6 + 6 = $ _____

1. Add.

$$4 + 5 = \underline{\hspace{1.5cm}}$$

- ○ 8
- ○ 9
- ○ 10
- ○ 11

3. What is the missing number?

$$9 + \underline{\hspace{1.5cm}} = 18$$

- ○ 7
- ○ 8
- ○ 9
- ○ 10

2. Subtract.

$$10 - 6 = \underline{\hspace{1.5cm}}$$

- ○ 6
- ○ 5
- ○ 4
- ○ 3

4. What is the missing number?

$$12 - \underline{\hspace{1.5cm}} = 7$$

- ○ 9
- ○ 7
- ○ 6
- ○ 5

PROBLEM SOLVING  REAL WORLD

Solve. Draw or write to explain.

5. Jesse has 4 shells. He finds some more. Now he has 12 shells. How many more shells did Jesse find?

_____ more shells

Lesson 42

COMMON CORE STANDARD CC.1.OA.7
Lesson Objective: Determine if an equation is true or false.

Algebra • Equal and Not Equal

An equal sign means both sides are the same.

$$3 + 3 = 6 - 0$$

THINK
$3 + 3 = 6$ and $6 - 0 = 6$.
Is 6 the same as 6?
yes

It is true.

$$3 + 2 = 5 - 2$$

THINK
$3 + 2 = 5$ and $5 - 2 = 3$.
Is 5 the same as 3?
no

It is false.

Which is true? Circle your answer.
Which is false? Cross out your answer.

1. $$7 - 5 = 5 - 2$$
   $$8 - 8 = 6 - 6$$

2. $$1 + 8 = 18$$
   $$2 + 8 = 8 + 2$$

3. $$4 + 3 = 5 + 2$$
   $$7 + 3 = 4 + 5$$

4. $$9 - 2 = 9 + 2$$
   $$9 = 10 - 1$$

1. Which makes the
   sentence true?

   $10 - 4 = 2 + \boxed{}$

   ○ 3
   ○ 4
   ○ 5
   ○ 6

3. Which makes the
   sentence true?

   $16 - 7 = 8 + \boxed{}$

   ○ 1
   ○ 2
   ○ 3
   ○ 4

2. Which makes the
   sentence true?

   $12 - 0 = 6 + \boxed{}$

   ○ 4
   ○ 5
   ○ 6
   ○ 7

4. Which makes the
   sentence true?

   $8 + 2 = \underline{}$

   ○ $10 - 1$
   ○ $5 + 5$
   ○ $13 - 4$
   ○ $3 + 8$

5. Write two numbers to make the sentence true.

   $8 + 6 = \underline{} + \underline{}$

Name _____

Lesson 43

COMMON CORE STANDARD CC.1.OA.8
Lesson Objective: Compare pictorial groups to understand subtraction.

Use Pictures and Subtraction to Compare

You can subtract to compare groups.

$$7 - 6 = \underline{}$$

There is I **more** ⊕
than there are 🗑.

There is I **fewer**
than there are ⊛.

Subtract to compare.

1.

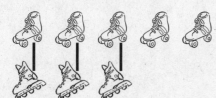

$$5 - 3 = \underline{}$$

_____ more

2.

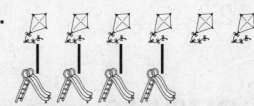

$$6 - 4 = \underline{}$$

_____ fewer 🪜

3.

$$4 - 1 = \underline{}$$

_____ more ◯

4.

$$7 - 3 = \underline{}$$

_____ fewer

1. How many fewer  are there?

4 − 3 = _____

○ I fewer   ○ 7 fewer

○ 4 fewer   ○ 8 fewer

---

2. How many more  are there?

6 − 2 = _____

○ 8 more   ○ 4 more

○ 6 more   ○ 2 more

PROBLEM SOLVING REAL WORLD

Draw a picture to show the problem.
Write a subtraction sentence to
match your picture.

3. Jo has 4 golf clubs and
   2 golf balls. How many fewer
   golf balls does Jo have?

_____ − _____ = _____   _____ fewer

Name _____

Lesson 44

COMMON CORE STANDARD CC.1.0A.8

Lesson Objective: Identify how many are
left when subtracting all or 0.

Subtract All or Zero

When you subtract zero from a
number, the difference is the
number.

No ⬤ are crossed out.

$4 - 0 =$ __4__

When you subtract a number from
itself, the difference
is zero.

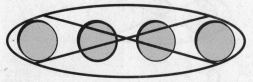

All ⬤ are crossed out.

$4 - 4 =$ __0__

Use ⬤. Write the difference.

1.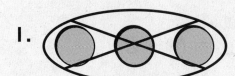

$3 - 3 =$ __0__

2.

$5 - 0 =$ ___

---

3. ⬤ ⬤

$2 - 0 =$ ___

4.

$1 - 1 =$ ___

5.

$6 - 0 =$ ___

6.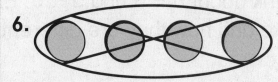

$4 - 4 =$ ___

---

1. Mary has 3 flowers. She gives 3 flowers to her mother. How many flowers does Mary have now?

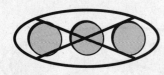

- ○ 0
- ○ 1
- ○ 2
- ○ 6

2. Carl has 7 grapes. He does not eat any grapes. How many grapes does Carl have left?

- ○ 17
- ○ 7
- ○ 5
- ○ 0

3. What is the difference?

$$9 - 0 = \underline{\quad}$$

- ○ 0
- ○ 1
- ○ 8
- ○ 9

4. What is the difference?

$$\underline{\quad} = 6 - 6$$

- ○ 12
- ○ 6
- ○ 3
- ○ 0

5. Think about $5 - 5$ and $5 - 0$. Explain how they are alike and how they are different.

_____

_____

Core Standards for Math, Grade 1

Name _____

Algebra • Missing Numbers

Add or subtract to find the missing numbers.

$6 + \boxed{5} = 11$

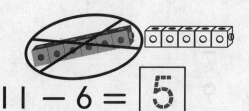

$11 - 6 = \boxed{5}$

THINK
I start with 6. I keep adding cubes until there are 11. The missing number is 5. A related fact is $11 - 6 = 5$.

Use  to find the missing numbers.

Write the numbers.

1.

$4 + \boxed{} = 13$

$13 - 4 = \boxed{}$

2.

$7 + \boxed{} = 15$

$15 - 7 = \boxed{}$

3.

$8 + \boxed{} = 14$

$14 - 8 = \boxed{}$

4.

$9 + \boxed{} = 16$

$16 - 9 = \boxed{}$

5.

$9 + \boxed{} = 18$

$18 - 9 = \boxed{}$

6.

$8 + \boxed{} = 16$

$16 - 8 = \boxed{}$

1. What is the missing number?

$$5 + \boxed{} = 13$$

$$13 - 5 = \boxed{}$$

- ○ 4
- ○ 5
- ○ 8
- ○ 9

2. What is the missing number?

$$4 + \boxed{} = 11$$

$$11 - 4 = \boxed{}$$

- ○ 11
- ○ 10
- ○ 8
- ○ 7

3. What is the missing number?

$$6 + \boxed{} = 15$$

$$15 - 6 = \boxed{}$$

- ○ 7
- ○ 9
- ○ 11
- ○ 21

4. What is the missing number?

$$8 + \boxed{} = 16$$

- ○ 1
- ○ 6
- ○ 8
- ○ 10

5. Write the missing number.

$$17 - 8 = \underline{}$$

Name _____

Lesson 46

COMMON CORE STANDARD CC.1.OA.8
Lesson Objective: Use a related fact to subtract.

Algebra • Use Related Facts

Find 11 − 6.

Use counters to help you.

THINK
Start with 6. How many do I add to make 11?

6 + _5_ = 11

11 − 6 = _5_

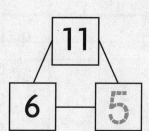

Use counters. Write the missing numbers.

1. Find 13 − 8.

8 + ___ = 13

13 − 8 = ___

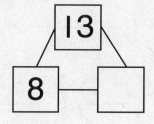

2. Find 12 − 3.

3 + ___ = 12

12 − 3 = ___

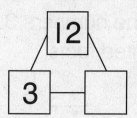

1. What is the missing number?

$$10 - 4 = \boxed{}$$

$$4 + \boxed{} = 10$$

○ 3   ○ 6
○ 4   ○ 7

2. What is the missing number?

$$12 - 6 = \boxed{}$$

$$6 + \boxed{} = 12$$

○ 4
○ 5
○ 6
○ 9

3. What is the missing number?

$$11 - 3 = \boxed{}$$

$$3 + \boxed{} = 11$$

○ 7   ○ 9
○ 8   ○ 11

4. Look at the shapes in the addition sentence. Which shape completes the related subtraction fact?

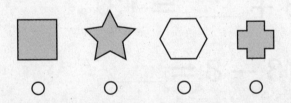

○   ○   ○   ○

5. Use the numbers 3, 9, and 12 to write 4 related facts.

___ + ___ = ___   ___ − ___ = ___

___ + ___ = ___   ___ − ___ = ___

Name _____

Lesson **47**

COMMON CORE STANDARD CC.1.NBT.1

Lesson Objective: Count by ones to extend a counting sequence up to 120.

Count by Ones to 120

1	2	3	4	5	6	7	8	9	10
11	12	13	14	15	16	17	18	19	20
21	22	23	24	25	26	27	28	29	30
31	32	33	34	35	36	37	38	39	40
41	42	43	44	45	46	47	48	49	50
51	52	53	54	55	56	57	58	59	60
61	62	63	64	65	66	67	68	69	70
71	72	73	74	75	76	77	78	79	80
81	82	83	84	85	86	87	88	89	90
91	92	93	94	95	96	97	98	99	100
101	102	103	104	105	106	107	108	109	110
111	112	113	114	115	116	117	118	119	120

Count forward.
Write the numbers.

I find **108** on the chart.
109 comes next.

108, _109_, _110_, _111_

Use a Counting Chart. Count forward.
Write the numbers.

1. 112, ___, ___, ___

2. 25, ___, ___, ___

3. 95, ___, ___, ___

4. 50, ___, ___, ___

Use the Counting Chart for 1–3.

1	2	3	4	5	6	7	8	9	10
11	12	13	14	15	16	17	18	19	20
21	22	23	24	25	26	27	28	29	30
31	32	33	34	35	36	37	38	39	40
41	42	43	44	45	46	47	48	49	50
51	52	53	54	55	56	57	58	59	60
61	62	63	64	65	66	67	68	69	70
71	72	73	74	75	76	77	78	79	80
81	82	83	84	85	86	87	88	89	90
91	92	93	94	95	96	97	98	99	100
101	102	103	104	105	106	107	108	109	110
111	112	113	114	115	116	117	118	119	120

1. Jane counted by saying 56, 57, 58, and 59.
   What are the next three numbers Jane will say?

   60, 61, 62   60, 65, 70   69, 79, 89   70, 71, 72
   ○   ○   ○   ○

2. Count forward. What number is missing?
   108, 109, 110, _____ 112

   120   113   111   101
   ○   ○   ○   ○

3. Cara has 78 pennies. Draw more pennies
   so there are 84 pennies in all. Write the
   numbers to count on to 84.

Name _____

Lesson 48
COMMON CORE STANDARD CC.1.NBT.1
Lesson Objective: Count by tens from any number to extend a counting sequence up to 120.

Count by Tens to 120

Use the Counting Chart.
Count forward by tens.
Start on 4.

14, 24, 34, 44, 54,

64, 74, <u>84</u>, <u>94</u>,

<u>104</u>, <u>114</u>

1	2	3	4	5	6	7	8	9	10
11	12	13	14	15	16	17	18	19	20
21	22	23	24	25	26	27	28	29	30
31	32	33	34	35	36	37	38	39	40
41	42	43	44	45	46	47	48	49	50
51	52	53	54	55	56	57	58	59	60
61	62	63	64	65	66	67	68	69	70
71	72	73	74	75	76	77	78	79	80
81	82	83	84	85	86	87	88	89	90
91	92	93	94	95	96	97	98	99	100
101	102	103	104	105	106	107	108	109	110
111	112	113	114	115	116	117	118	119	120

Use the Counting Chart to count by tens.
Write the numbers.

1. Start on 5.

15, 25, 35, 45, ___, ___, ___, ___, ___

2. Start on 38.

48, 58, 68, ___, ___, ___, ___, ___, ___

3. Start on 26.

36, 46, ___, ___, ___, ___, ___, ___

Use the Counting Chart for 1–4.

1	2	3	4	5	6	7	8	9	10
11	12	13	14	15	16	17	18	19	20
21	22	23	24	25	26	27	28	29	30
31	32	33	34	35	36	37	38	39	40
41	42	43	44	45	46	47	48	49	50
51	52	53	54	55	56	57	58	59	60
61	62	63	64	65	66	67	68	69	70
71	72	73	74	75	76	77	78	79	80
81	82	83	84	85	86	87	88	89	90
91	92	93	94	95	96	97	98	99	100
101	102	103	104	105	106	107	108	109	110
111	112	113	114	115	116	117	118	119	120

1. Count by tens. What number is missing?

25, 35, 45, _____, 65

46   55   50   66
○   ○   ○   ○

2. Start on 24. Count by tens. What is the **last** number you will say that is on the Counting Chart?

30   104   114   120
○   ○   ○   ○

3. Count by tens. What number comes next?

30, 40, 50, _____

75   70   65   60
○   ○   ○   ○

4. What does it mean to count by tens? Explain.

_____

_____

Name _____

Lesson 49

COMMON CORE STANDARD CC.1.NBT.1

Lesson Objective: Read and write numerals to represent a number of 100 to 110 objects.

Model, Read, and Write Numbers from 100 to 110

What is 10 tens and 2 more?

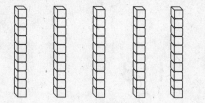

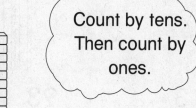

Count by tens. Then count by ones.

10, 20, 30, 40, 50, 60, 70, 80, 90, _100_, _101_, _102_

10 tens and 2 more = _102_

Use [rod] [cube] to model the number.
Write the number.

1. 10 tens and 3 more

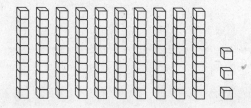

_____

2. 10 tens and 7 more

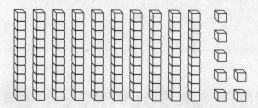

_____

3. 10 tens and 6 more

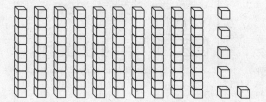

_____

4. 10 tens and 9 more

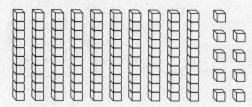

_____

1. What number does the model show?

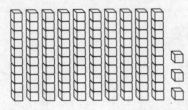

13   93   103   113
○   ○   ○   ○

2. Which number has 10 tens and 5 more?

115   105   95   15
○   ○   ○   ○

3. Which number has 10 tens and 9 ones?

109   108   106   91
○   ○   ○   ○

PROBLEM SOLVING

4. Solve to find the number of pens.

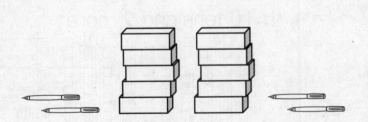

THINK

✎ = 1 pen

▭ = 10 pens

There are _____ pens.

Name _____

Lesson 50

COMMON CORE STANDARD CC.1.NBT.1
Lesson Objective: Read and write numerals to represent a number of 110 to 120 objects.

Model, Read, and Write Numbers from 110 to 120

What is the number?

Count by tens.
Then count by ones.

10 20 30 40 50 60 70 80 90 100 110 111 112 113

The number is ___113___.

Use ▭ ◻ to model the number.
Write the number.

1.

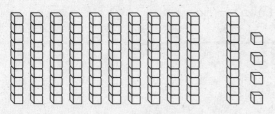

_____

2.

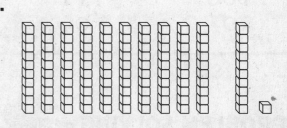

_____

3.

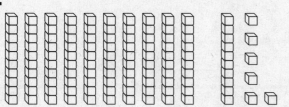

_____

4.

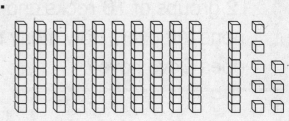

_____

1. What number does the model show?

15   105   111   115
○   ○   ○   ○

---

2. Which number means the same as 12 tens?

120   112   110   102
○   ○   ○   ○

---

3. Which number means the same as 11 tens and 3 ones?

103   111   113   114
○   ○   ○   ○

PROBLEM SOLVING

Choose a way to solve. Draw or write to explain.

4. Dave collects rocks. He makes
   12 groups of 10 rocks and has
   none left over. How many rocks
   does Dave have?   _____ rocks

Name _____

Lesson 51

COMMON CORE STANDARD CC.1.NBT.2
Lesson Objective: Group objects to show numbers to 50 as tens and ones.

Tens and Ones to 50

You can use tens and ones
to show a number.

There are 4 tens.
There are 2 ones.
This shows 42.

Tens	Ones

4 tens   2 ones = __42__

Use ⬚⬚⬚⬚⬚⬚⬚⬚ ▱ **to show the tens and ones.**
Write the numbers.

1.

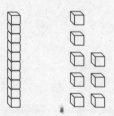

1 tens 8 ones = __18__

2.

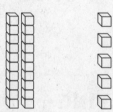

2 tens 5 ones = _____

3.

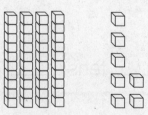

4 tens 7 ones = _____

4.

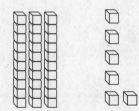

3 tens 6 ones = _____

Core Standards for Math, Grade 1

Name _____

1. How many tens and ones are shown?

○ 3 tens 5 ones
○ 4 tens 5 ones
○ 5 tens 4 ones
○ 6 tens 4 ones

2. Which number does the model show?

○ 63
○ 38
○ 36
○ 26

PROBLEM SOLVING

Solve. Write the numbers.

3. I have 43 cubes. How many tens and ones can I make?

_____ tens _____ ones

Name _____

Lesson 52

COMMON CORE STANDARD CC.1.NBT.2

Lesson Objective: Group objects to show numbers to 100 as tens and ones.

Tens and Ones to 100

If you know the tens and ones,
you can write the number.

There are 9 tens.
There are 8 ones.
The number is 98.

Tens	Ones

9 tens   8 ones = __98__

Use ▭ ▱ to show the tens and ones.
Write the numbers.

1.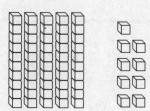

5 tens 9 ones = __59__

2.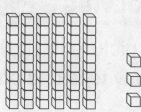

6 tens 3 ones = _____

3.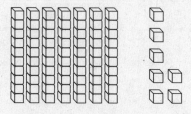

7 tens 7 ones = _____

4.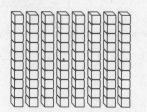

8 tens 2 ones = _____

Core Standards for Math, Grade 1

1. What number does the model show?

○ 16   ○ 61

○ 17   ○ 67

2. Mr. Lee's oak tree is 83 years old. How many tens and ones are in 83?

○ 11 tens 0 ones

○ 8 tens 3 ones

○ 8 tens 2 ones

○ 3 tens 8 ones

PROBLEM SOLVING  REAL WORLD

Draw a quick picture to show the number.
Write how many tens and ones there are.

3. Inez has 57 shells.

_____ tens _____ ones

Problem Solving • Show Numbers in Different Ways

How can you show the number 34 two different ways?

Unlock the Problem

What do I need to find?	**What information do I need to use?**
two different ways to show a number	The number is 34.

Show how to solve the problem.

> **THINK**
> You can trade I ten for I0 ones.

First Way		**Second Way**	
Tens	**Ones**	**Tens**	**Ones**

I. Use ▭ ▱ to show 26 two different ways. Draw both ways.

Tens	**Ones**

Tens	**Ones**

1. Which is a different way to show
the same number?

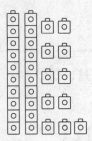 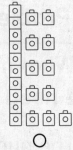 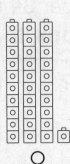 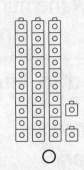 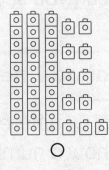

        ○   ○   ○   ○

2. Which number is the same as 3 tens and 22 ones?

  23   32   42   52
  ○   ○   ○   ○

3. Which number is the same as 5 tens and 6 ones?

  46   55   56   66
  ○   ○   ○   ○

4. Think of a number greater than 30. Your
number should have two different digits. Write
your number. Then make quick pictures to
show your number three ways.

First way | Second way | Third way

My number is _____ .

Name _____

Lesson 54

COMMON CORE STANDARD CC.1.NBT.2b
Lesson Objective: Use models and write to
represent equivalent forms of ten and ones.

Understand Ten and Ones

You can use 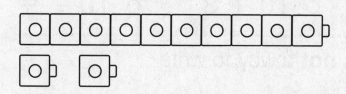 to show ten and some ones.
You can write ten and ones in different ways.

___1___ ten ___2___ ones

___10___ + ___2___

___12___

Use the model. Write the number three different ways.

1.
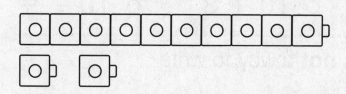 _____ ten _____ ones

_____ + _____

_____

2. 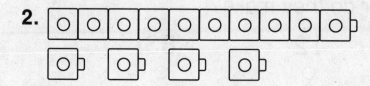 _____ ten _____ ones

_____ + _____

_____

3. 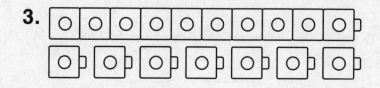 _____ ten _____ ones

_____ + _____

_____

Name _____

1. Which shows the same number?

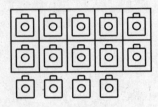

    ○ 10 + 4   ○ 10

    ○ 10 + 3   ○ 10 − 4

2. Look at the model. Which is **not** a way to write
the number?

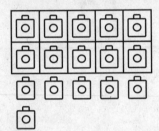

    ○ 1 ten 6 ones

    ○ 10 + 6

    ○ 16

    ○ 61

3. Which number means the same as 1 ten 9 ones?

   109   91   19   16
    ○   ○   ○   ○

4. Pam has 8 ones. Bo has 3 ones. They put all their
ones together. What number do they make?

    5   11   12   83
    ○   ○   ○   ○

5. Use the model. Write the number three
different ways.

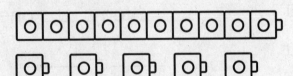

_____ ten _____ ones

_____ + _____

_____

Lesson 55

COMMON CORE STANDARD CC.1.NBT.2b
Lesson Objective: Use objects, pictures, and numbers to represent a ten and some ones.

Make Ten and Ones

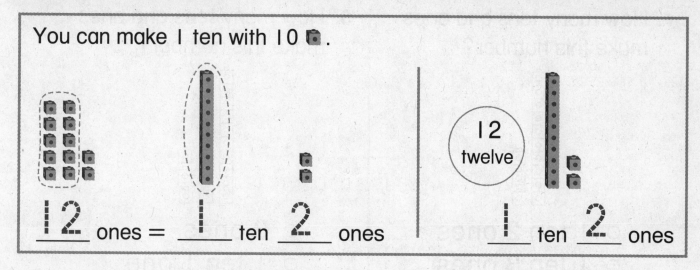

You can make 1 ten with 10 ⬛ .

___12___ ones = ___1___ ten ___2___ ones

12 twelve

___1___ ten ___2___ ones

Write how many tens and ones.

1.

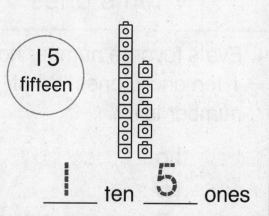

15 fifteen

___1___ ten ___5___ ones

2.

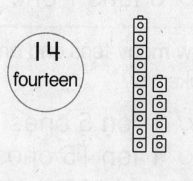

14 fourteen

_____ ten _____ ones

3.

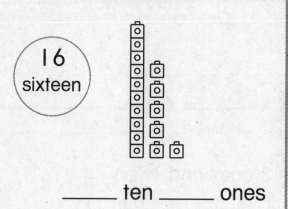

16 sixteen

_____ ten _____ ones

4.

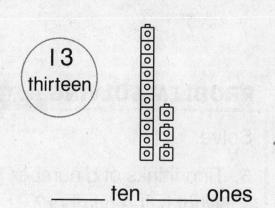

13 thirteen

_____ ten _____ ones

Core Standards for Math, Grade 1

1. How many tens and ones make this number?

○ 1 ten 2 ones
○ 1 ten 3 ones
○ 1 ten 8 ones
○ 3 tens 1 one

3. How many tens and ones make this number?

○ 8 ones
○ 1 ten 1 one
○ 1 ten 7 ones
○ 1 ten 8 ones

2. How many tens and ones make 15?

○ 1 ten 5 ones
○ 1 ten 15 ones
○ 1 ten 10 ones
○ 5 tens 1 one

4. Eve's favorite number has 1 ten and 6 ones. What number is it?

○ 16
○ 10
○ 7
○ 6

PROBLEM SOLVING

Solve.

5. Tina thinks of a number that has 3 ones and 1 ten.
What is the number?

_____

Core Standards for Math, Grade 1

Name _____

Lesson 56

COMMON CORE STANDARD CC.1.NBT.2c

Lesson Objective: Use objects, pictures, and
numbers to represent tens.

Tens

You can put **ones** together
to make **tens**.

Draw to show the 2 tens.

20 ones = 2 tens

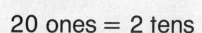

<u> 2 </u> tens = <u> 20 </u>

Use . Make groups of ten. Draw the tens.
Write how many tens. Write the number.

1.

30 ones = 3 tens

_____ tens = _____

2.

40 ones = 4 tens

_____ tens = _____

3.

50 ones = 5 tens

_____ tens = _____

1. What number does the model show?

○ 50
○ 40
○ 20
○ 10

3. What number does the model show?

○ 40
○ 50
○ 60
○ 70

2. What number means 80 ones?

○ 8
○ 18
○ 80
○ 81

4. Which is true?

○ 2 tens = 12
○ 3 tens = 33
○ 5 tens = 50
○ 9 tens = 99

PROBLEM SOLVING REAL WORLD

Look at the model. Write the number.

5. What number does the model show?

_____

Name _____

Lesson 57

COMMON CORE STANDARD CC.1.NBT.3

Lesson Objective: Model and compare two-digit numbers to determine which is greater.

Algebra • Greater Than

You can compare numbers to find which is greater.

48

24

____ is greater than ____ .

48 > 24

65

62

____ is greater than ____ .

65 > 62

Draw lines to match.

Write the numbers to compare.

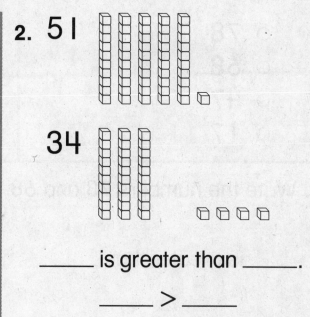

1. 43

55

____ is greater than ____ .

____ > ____

2. 51

34

____ is greater than ____ .

____ > ____

1. Jessica counts 22 stars. The number of stars that Tim counts is **greater than** 22. Which could be a number of stars Tim counts?

   ○ 24
   ○ 21
   ○ 20
   ○ 18

2. Which number is **greater than** 74?

   ○ 78
   ○ 68
   ○ 47
   ○ 17

3. Which number is **greater than** 91?

   ○ 19
   ○ 90
   ○ 91
   ○ 95

4. The number of pens that Jill has is **greater than** 38. Which could be a number of pens Jill has?

   ○ 11
   ○ 27
   ○ 37
   ○ 43

5. Write the numbers 73 and 68 to make the sentence true.

   _____ is greater than _____ .

Name _____

Lesson 58

COMMON CORE STANDARD CC.1.NBT.3

Lesson Objective: Model and compare
two-digit numbers to determine which is less.

Algebra • Less Than

You can compare numbers to
find which is less.

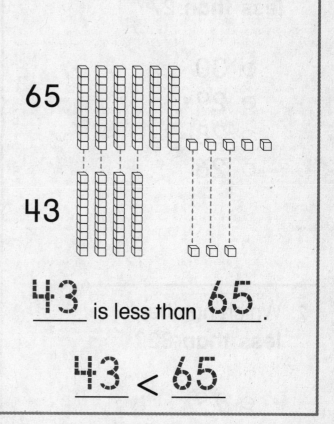

23 _____ is less than _____ 26 .

$$\underline{23} < \underline{26}$$

43 _____ is less than _____ 65 .

$$\underline{43} < \underline{65}$$

Draw lines to match.
Write the numbers to compare.

1.

37

31

_____ is less than _____.

$$\underline{} < \underline{}$$

2.

74

44

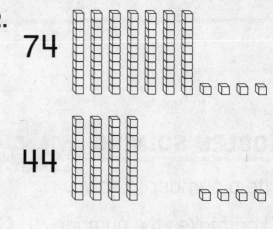

_____ is less than _____.

$$\underline{} < \underline{}$$

Name _____

1. Which number is **less than** 27?

- ○ 30
- ○ 29
- ○ 28
- ○ 26

2. Which number is **less than** 82?

- ○ 79
- ○ 85
- ○ 89
- ○ 91

3. Jonathon has 42 marbles. The number of marbles that Kris has is **less than** 42. Which could be a number of marbles Kris has?

- ○ 40
- ○ 43
- ○ 46
- ○ 52

4. The number of ducks that Mark sees is **less than** 22. Which could be a number of ducks Mark sees?

- ○ 52
- ○ 31
- ○ 23
- ○ 17

PROBLEM SOLVING

Write a number to solve.

5. Lori makes the number 74. Gabe makes a number that is less than 74. What could be a number Gabe makes? _____

Name _____

Lesson 59

COMMON CORE STANDARD CC.1.NBT.3

Lesson Objective: Use symbols for *is less than* "<", *is greater than* ">", and *is equal to* "=" to compare numbers.

Algebra • Use Symbols to Compare

You can use symbols to compare numbers.

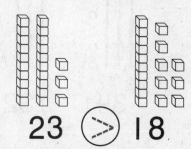

15 < 18
18 = 18
23 > 18

| This symbol means **is less than.** | This symbol means **is equal to.** | This symbol means **is greater than.** |

Write >, <, or =. Complete the sentence.

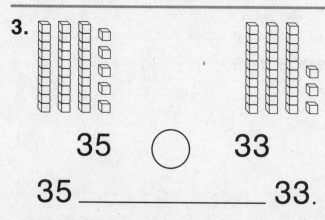

1.
51 < 57
51 _is less than_ 57.

2.
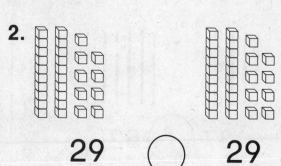
29 ◯ 29
29 _____ 29.

3.
35 ◯ 33
35 _____ 33.

4.
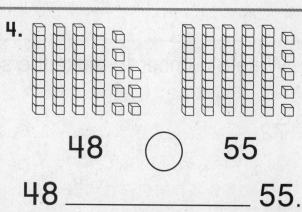
48 ◯ 55
48 _____ 55.

1. Which symbol is missing?

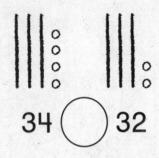

34 ◯ 32

<   >   =
◦   ◦   ◦

2. Which symbol is missing?

37 ◯ 52

<   >   =
◦   ◦   ◦

3. Which is true?

51 ◯ 44

◦ 51 = 44
◦ 51 > 44
◦ 51 < 44
◦ 44 > 51

4. Which is true?

◦ 61 < 58
◦ 61 = 58
◦ 58 > 61
◦ 61 > 58

5. Write a number to make the sentence true.

72 < _____

Name _____

Lesson 60

COMMON CORE STANDARD CC.1.NBT.3
Lesson Objective: Solve problems using the
strategy *make a model*.

Problem Solving • Compare Numbers

Anthony has the number cards
shown. He gives away the cards
with numbers less than 6 and greater
than 9. Which cards does Anthony have now?

Unlock the Problem

What do I need to find?	What information do I need to use?
the <u>number cards</u> that Anthony has now	number cards < ___6___ and > ___9___.

Show how to solve the problem.

> **THINK**
> Cross out the numbers
> Anthony gives away.

Anthony has number cards ___7___ and ___8___.

Make a model to solve.

1. Emily has the number cards shown.
   She gives away the cards less
   than 19 and greater than 22.
   Which cards does she have now?

Emily has _____ and _____.

1. Erin has these number cards. She gives away the cards with numbers less than 85 and greater than 88. Which cards does Erin have now?

| 82 | 84 | 86 | 87 | 89 |

- ○ 84, 86
- ○ 86, 87
- ○ 82, 89
- ○ 84, 89

2. Stephen has these number cards. He keeps the cards with numbers less than 28 and greater than 24. Which cards does Stephen keep?

| 22 | 23 | 25 | 27 | 29 |

- ○ 22, 25
- ○ 23, 27
- ○ 25, 27
- ○ 27, 29

3. Cody circles the numbers greater than 54 and underlines the numbers less than 61. Which numbers are both greater than 54 and less than 61?

| 51 | 53 | 56 | 59 | 63 | 66 |

- ○ 56, 59
- ○ 56, 63
- ○ 51, 59
- ○ 53, 63

4. Michelle picks up the number cards that are greater than 41 and less than 45. Which number cards does Michelle pick up?

| 39 | 42 | 44 | 46 | 49 |

- ○ 42, 44
- ○ 39, 44
- ○ 44, 49
- ○ 39, 42

5. Sue crossed out the numbers that are less than 91 and greater than 96. Circle the number that is left.

| 90 | 95 | 97 |

| 98 | 99 |

Name _____

Lesson 61

COMMON CORE STANDARD CC.1.NBT.4
Lesson Objective: Draw a model to add tens.

Add Tens

What is $10 + 30$?

| | | |

Use ▭▭▭.
Start with 1 ten.
Add 3 more tens.
Draw the tens.

1 ten + 3 tens = __4__ tens

$10 + 30 =$ __40__

Use ▭▭▭. Draw to show tens.
Write how many tens. Write the sum.

1.

1 ten + 8 tens = ____ tens

$10 + 80 =$ ____

2.

4 tens + 3 tens = ____ tens

$40 + 30 =$ ____

3.

2 tens + 6 tens = ____ tens

$20 + 60 =$ ____

4.

5 tens + 3 tens = ____ tens

$50 + 30 =$ ____

1. How many tens are in the sum?

$$50 + 10 = 60$$

- ○ 1 ten
- ○ 5 tens
- ○ 6 tens
- ○ 7 tens

2. How many tens are in the sum?

$$20 + 60 = 80$$

- ○ 2 tens
- ○ 6 tens
- ○ 7 tens
- ○ 8 tens

3. What is the sum?

$$70 + 20 = \_\_\_\_$$

- ○ 9
- ○ 50
- ○ 80
- ○ 90

4. What is the sum?

$$30 + 40 = \_\_\_\_$$

- ○ 7
- ○ 10
- ○ 70
- ○ 80

5. Draw groups of tens you can add to get a sum of 70. Write the number sentence.

Name _____

Lesson 62

COMMON CORE STANDARD CC.1.NBT.4
Lesson Objective: Use a hundred chart to find sums.

Use a Hundred Chart to Add

You can count on to add on a hundred chart.

1	2	3	4	5	6	7	8	9	10
11	12	13	14	15	16	17	18	19	20
21	22	23	24	25	26	27	28	29	30
31	32	33	34	35	36	37	38	39	40
41	42	43	44	45	46	47	48	49	50
51	52	53	54	55	56	57	58	59	60
61	62	63	64	65	66	67	68	69	70
71	72	73	74	75	76	77	78	79	80
81	82	83	84	85	86	87	88	89	90
91	92	93	94	95	96	97	98	99	100

Start at 21. Move right to count on 3 ones. Count

22 , 23 , 24

$21 + 3 = 24$

Start at 68. Move down to count on 3 tens. Count

78 , 88 , 98

$68 + 30 = 98$

Use the hundred chart to add.

Count on by ones.

1. $46 + 2 = $ _____

2. $63 + 3 = $ _____

Count on by tens.

3. $52 + 30 = $ _____

4. $23 + 40 = $ _____

Use the hundred chart for 1–3.

1	2	3	4	5	6	7	8	9	10
11	12	13	14	15	16	17	18	19	20
21	22	23	24	25	26	27	28	29	30
31	32	33	34	35	36	37	38	39	40
41	42	43	44	45	46	47	48	49	50
51	52	53	54	55	56	57	58	59	60
61	62	63	64	65	66	67	68	69	70
71	72	73	74	75	76	77	78	79	80
81	82	83	84	85	86	87	88	89	90
91	92	93	94	95	96	97	98	99	100

2. Use the hundred chart to add. Count on by tens.

$$67 + 30 = \underline{\hspace{1cm}}$$

○ 97   ○ 87
○ 70   ○ 37

1. Use the hundred chart to add. Count on by ones.

$$45 + 4 = \underline{\hspace{1cm}}$$

○ 38   ○ 49
○ 48   ○ 59

3. Use the hundred chart to add. Count on by tens.

$$20 + 51 = \underline{\hspace{1cm}}$$

○ 71   ○ 31
○ 70   ○ 30

4. Add. Show your work on the hundred chart.

$$23 + 40 + 10 = \underline{\hspace{1cm}}$$

1	2	3	4	5	6	7	8	9	10
11	12	13	14	15	16	17	18	19	20
21	22	23	24	25	26	27	28	29	30
31	32	33	34	35	36	37	38	39	40
41	42	43	44	45	46	47	48	49	50
51	52	53	54	55	56	57	58	59	60
61	62	63	64	65	66	67	68	69	70
71	72	73	74	75	76	77	78	79	80
81	82	83	84	85	86	87	88	89	90
91	92	93	94	95	96	97	98	99	100

Name _____

Lesson 63

COMMON CORE STANDARD CC.1.NBT.4
Lesson Objective: Use concrete models to
add ones or tens to a two-digit number.

Use Models to Add

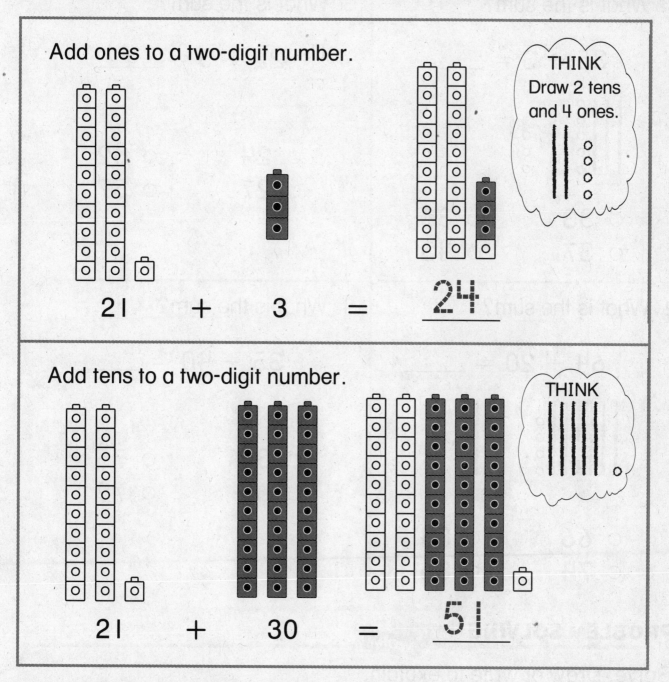

Add ones to a two-digit number.

THINK
Draw 2 tens
and 4 ones.

21   +   3   =   24

Add tens to a two-digit number.

THINK

21   +   30   =   51

Use ▢. Draw to show how to add the
ones or tens. Write the sum.

1. $15 + 2 =$ _____

2. $15 + 20 =$ _____

Core Standards for Math, Grade 1

1. What is the sum?

$$35 + 3 = \underline{\hspace{1cm}}$$

- ○ 33
- ○ 37
- ○ 38
- ○ 43

2. What is the sum?

$$64 + 20 = \underline{\hspace{1cm}}$$

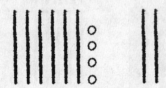

- ○ 66
- ○ 74
- ○ 84
- ○ 86

3. What is the sum?

$$22 + 5 = \underline{\hspace{1cm}}$$

- ○ 24
- ○ 27
- ○ 52
- ○ 57

4. What is the sum?

$$35 + 40 = \underline{\hspace{1cm}}$$

- ○ 39
- ○ 65
- ○ 75
- ○ 79

PROBLEM SOLVING

Solve. Draw or write to explain.

5. Maria has 21 marbles.
   She buys a bag of 20 marbles.
   How many marbles does
   Maria have now?

   _____ marbles

Lesson 64

COMMON CORE STANDARD CC.1.NBT.4

Lesson Objective: Make a ten to add a two-digit number and a one-digit number.

Make Ten to Add

What is 17 + 5?

Step 1

Use ⬤.

Show 17.

Use ◯.

Show 5.

Step 2

Make
a
ten.

Step 3 Add.

$$20 + 2 = \underline{22}$$

$$\text{So, } 17 + 5 = \underline{22}.$$

Draw to show how you make a ten. Find the sum.

1. What is 16 + 8?

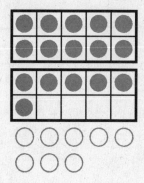

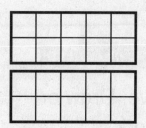

$$\underline{20} + \underline{4} = \underline{24}$$

$$\text{So, } 16 + 8 = \underline{}.$$

Name _____

1. Make a ten to find the sum.

$$34 + 7 = \underline{\quad}$$

○ 31   ○ 42
○ 41   ○ 46

3. What is $28 + 4$?

○ 24
○ 30
○ 32
○ 34

2. Make a ten to find the sum.

$$52 + 9 = \underline{\quad}$$

○ 51   ○ 62
○ 61   ○ 72

4. What is $79 + 6$?

○ 84
○ 85
○ 86
○ 87

PROBLEM SOLVING

Choose a way to solve. Draw or write to show your work.

5. Debbie has 27 markers. Sal has 9 markers. How many markers do they have?

_____ markers

Name _____

Lesson 65

COMMON CORE STANDARD CC.1.NBT.4

Lesson Objective: Use tens and ones to add two-digit numbers.

Use Place Value to Add

You can use tens and ones to help you add.

Add 25 and 22.

Show 25. ⟶

Show 22. ⟶

Tens	Ones

How many tens? 2 tens + 2 tens = ___4___ tens

How many ones? 5 ones + 2 ones = ___7___ ones

___4___ tens + ___7___ ones

___40___ + ___7___ = ___47___

$$\begin{array}{r} 25 \\ + 22 \\ \hline 47 \end{array}$$

Use tens and ones to add.

1. Add 34 and 42.

Tens	Ones

3 tens + 4 tens = _____ tens

4 ones + 2 ones = _____ ones

_____ tens + _____ ones

_____ + _____ = _____

$$\begin{array}{r} 34 \\ + 42 \\ \hline \end{array}$$

Core Standards for Math, Grade 1

1. Use tens and ones to add.

$$42 \quad 4 \text{ tens} + 2 \text{ ones}$$
$$+ 15 \quad 1 \text{ ten} \ + 5 \text{ ones}$$

○ 27 = 2 tens + 7 ones
○ 37 = 3 tens + 7 ones
○ 47 = 4 tens + 7 ones
○ 57 = 5 tens + 7 ones

3. How many tens and ones are in the sum?

$$81$$
$$+ 13$$

○ 7 tens + 2 ones
○ 7 tens + 4 ones
○ 9 tens + 3 ones
○ 9 tens + 4 ones

2. Use tens and ones to add.

$$27 \quad 2 \text{ tens} + 7 \text{ ones}$$
$$+ 31 \quad 3 \text{ tens} + 1 \text{ one}$$

○ 58 = 5 tens + 8 ones
○ 68 = 6 tens + 8 ones
○ 95 = 9 tens + 5 ones
○ 50 = 5 tens + 0 ones

4. How many tens and ones are in the sum?

$$45$$
$$+ 21$$

○ 6 tens + 1 one
○ 6 tens + 5 ones
○ 6 tens + 6 ones
○ 7 tens + 1 one

5. Use tens and ones to add.

37 + 15

37 + _____ + 12

_____ + 12 = _____

So, 37 + 15 = _____

Name _____

Lesson 66

COMMON CORE STANDARD CC.1.NBT.4

Lesson Objective: Solve and explain two-digit addition word problems using the strategy *draw a picture*.

Problem Solving • Addition
Word Problems

Morgan plants 17 seeds.

Amy plants 8 seeds.

How many seeds do they plant?

Unlock the Problem

What do I need to find?	What information do I need to use?
how many <u>seeds</u> they plant	Morgan plants <u>17</u> seeds. Amy plants <u>8</u> seeds.

Show how to solve the problem.

count on ones

(make a ten)

add tens and ones

_____ seeds.

Draw to solve. Circle your reasoning.

1. Edward buys 24 tomato plants.

   He buys 15 pepper plants.

   How many plants does he buy?

   count on tens

   make a ten

   add tens and ones

   _____ plants

© Houghton Mifflin Harcourt Publishing Company

Core Standards for Math, Grade 1

1. Lin picks 12 apples.
   Pete picks 7 apples.
   Which number sentence
   shows how many apples
   they pick?

   ○ $7 + 5 = 12$
   ○ $7 + 7 = 14$
   ○ $12 + 5 = 17$
   ○ $12 + 7 = 19$

2. Jay has 41 trading cards.
   Mel has 24 trading cards.
   Which number sentence
   shows how many trading
   cards they have?

   ○ $24 + 17 = 41$
   ○ $24 + 24 = 48$
   ○ $24 + 41 = 65$
   ○ $41 + 17 = 58$

3. Paul finds 35 shells.
   Then he finds 20 more
   shells. How many shells
   does Paul find?

   ○ 50
   ○ 55
   ○ 60
   ○ 65

4. Shondra uses 64 beads
   for a necklace. Then she
   uses 26 beads for another
   necklace. How many beads
   does Shondra use?

   ○ 38
   ○ 80
   ○ 82
   ○ 90

5. Yuko recycles 17 bottles. Til recycles 8 bottles.
   How many bottles do they recycle?

   _____ bottles

   Tell how you found your answer.

   _____

Lesson 67

COMMON CORE STANDARD CC.1.NBT.5
Lesson Objective: Identify numbers that are
10 less or 10 more than a given number.

10 Less, 10 More

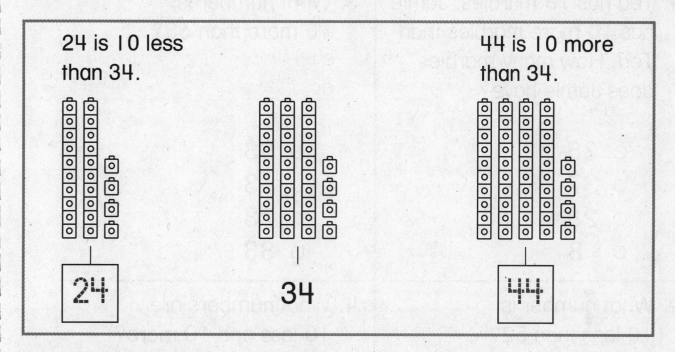

24 is 10 less
than 34.

44 is 10 more
than 34.

Write the numbers that are
10 less and 10 more.

1.

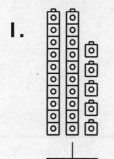

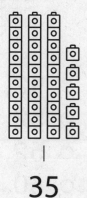

35

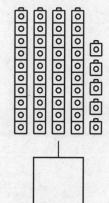

2.

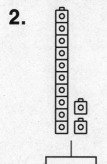

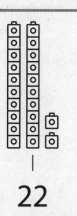

22

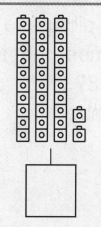

1. Ted has 18 marbles. Jamie has 10 more marbles than Ted. How many marbles does Jamie have?

   ○ 38
   ○ 37
   ○ 28
   ○ 8

2. What number is 10 less than 52?

   ○ 62
   ○ 52
   ○ 51
   ○ 42

3. What number is 10 more than 63?

   ○ 53
   ○ 63
   ○ 73
   ○ 83

4. What numbers are 10 less and 10 more?

   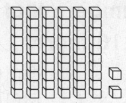

   ○ 42, 52
   ○ 52, 72
   ○ 52, 62
   ○ 60, 70

5. Draw a quick picture to show the number that is 10 less than 87. Write the number.

   ____

Name _____

Lesson 68

COMMON CORE STANDARD CC.1.NBT.6
Lesson Objective: Draw a model to subtract tens.

Subtract Tens

What is 60 − 40?

6 tens − 4 tens = __2__ tens

60 − 40 = __20__

Use ▭▭▭▭. Show 6 tens. Take away 4 tens. 2 tens are left.

Use ▭▭▭▭. Draw to show tens.
Write how many tens. Write the difference.

1.

7 tens − 4 tens = _____ tens

70 − 40 = _____

2.

9 tens − 5 tens = _____ tens

90 − 50 = _____

3.

5 tens − 2 tens = _____ tens

50 − 20 = _____

4.

8 tens − 7 tens = _____ ten

80 − 70 = _____

1. How many tens are in the difference?

$$60 - 10 = 50$$

- ○ 1 ten
- ○ 4 tens
- ○ 5 tens
- ○ 6 tens

2. How many tens are in the difference?

$$80 - 40 = 40$$

- ○ 8 tens
- ○ 6 tens
- ○ 5 tens
- ○ 4 tens

3. What is the difference?

$$70 - 30 = \underline{\hspace{1cm}}$$

- ○ 10
- ○ 20
- ○ 30
- ○ 40

4. What is the difference?

$$40 - 20 = \underline{\hspace{1cm}}$$

- ○ 60
- ○ 40
- ○ 20
- ○ 10

5. Kim has 50 strawberries. She gives some to Andy. She has 30 strawberries left. How many strawberries did Kim give to Andy?

_____ strawberries

Name _____

Lesson 69

COMMON CORE STANDARD CC.1.NBT.6
Lesson Objective: Add and subtract within 100, including continued practice with facts within 20.

Practice Addition and Subtraction

You can use models to add and subtract.

$$13 + 5 = \underline{18}$$

$$90 - 60 = \underline{30}$$

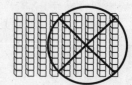

Add or subtract.

1. $33 + 6 = $ ___	2. $10 + 10 = $ ___	3. $15 - 8 = $ ___
4. $6 + 7 = $ ___	5. $54 + 23 = $ ___	6. $71 + 8 = $ ___
7. $5 + 5 = $ ___	8. $8 - 8 = $ ___	9. $16 + 3 = $ ___
10. $55 + 12 = $ ___	11. $9 - 7 = $ ___	12. $30 - 10 = $ ___

Name _____

1. Make a ten to find the sum.

$$8 + 6 = \underline{}$$

$$8 + 2 + 4$$

$$10 + 4$$

- ○ 14
- ○ 40
- ○ 41
- ○ 86

3. What is the sum?

$$33$$
$$+ 15$$

- ○ 42
- ○ 47
- ○ 48
- ○ 58

2. What is the difference?

$$60 - 40 = \underline{}$$

6 tens − 4 tens

- ○ 10
- ○ 20
- ○ 30
- ○ 40

4. What is the difference?

$$70 - 70 = \underline{}$$

- ○ 0
- ○ 7
- ○ 10
- ○ 77

5. Write 3 ways to get a difference of 15.

$$\underline{} - \underline{} = \underline{15}$$

$$\underline{} - \underline{} = \underline{15}$$

$$\underline{} - \underline{} = \underline{15}$$

Order Length

You can put objects in order by length.

These pencils are in order from **shortest** to **longest**.

shortest

longest

These pencils are in order from **longest** to **shortest**.

longest

shortest

Draw three lines in order from **shortest** to **longest**.

1. shortest |

2. |

3. longest |

Draw three lines in order from **longest** to **shortest**.

4. longest |

5. |

6. shortest |

1. Which ribbon is
   the shortest?

   ○

   ○

   ○

   ○

3. Which pencil is
   the longest?

   ○

   ○

   ○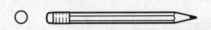

   ○

2. Which string is
   the shortest?

   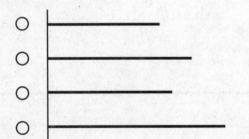

4. Which cube train is
   the longest?

   ○

   ○

   ○

   ○

PROBLEM SOLVING REAL WORLD

Solve.

5. Fred has the shortest
   toothbrush in the bathroom.
   Circle Fred's toothbrush.

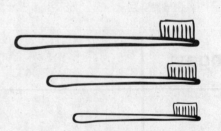

Lesson 71

COMMON CORE STANDARD CC.1.MD.1
Lesson Objective: Use the transitivity principle to measure indirectly.

Indirect Measurement

Clue 1: A marker is shorter than a pencil.

Clue 2: The pencil is shorter than a ribbon.

Is the marker shorter or longer than the ribbon?

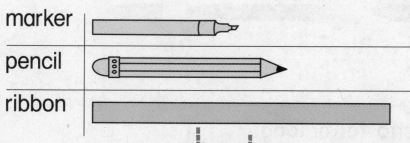

Draw Clue 1.
Draw Clue 2.
Then compare the marker and the ribbon.

So, the marker is ___shorter___ than the ribbon.

Use the clues. Write **shorter** or **longer** to complete the sentence. Then draw to prove your answer.

Draw Clue 1.
Draw Clue 2.
Then compare the string and the pencil.

1. Clue 1: A string is longer than a straw.

   Clue 2: The straw is longer than a pencil.

   Is the string shorter or longer than the pencil?

string

straw

pencil

The string is _____ than the pencil.

1. A white crayon is shorter than a gray crayon.
The gray crayon is shorter than a black crayon.
Which is correct?

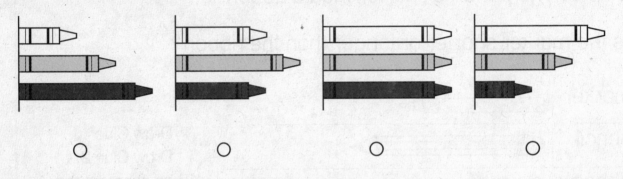

⭘   ⭘   ⭘   ⭘

2. Use the clues. Circle **shorter** or **longer**
to complete the sentence. Then draw
to prove your answer.

Clue 1: A blue line is shorter than a red line.
Clue 2: The red line is shorter than a green line.

So, the blue line is   shorter   than the green line.

                             longer

blue	
red	
green	

Name _____

Lesson 72

COMMON CORE STANDARD CC.1.MD.2
Lesson Objective: Measure length using nonstandard units.

Use Nonstandard Units
to Measure Length

You can use to measure length.

Line up the .

Count how many.

about ___5___

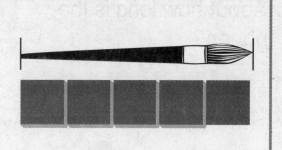

Use real objects. Use to measure.
Count how many.

1.

about _____

2.

about _____

3.

about _____

4.

about _____

Core Standards for Math, Grade 1

Use ▪ measuring 1 inch on each side to measure.

1. About how long is the ribbon?

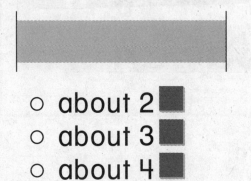

- ○ about 2 ▪
- ○ about 3 ▪
- ○ about 4 ▪
- ○ about 5 ▪

2. About how long is the paper clip?

- ○ about 1 ▪
- ○ about 2 ▪
- ○ about 3 ▪
- ○ about 4 ▪

3. About how long is the pencil?

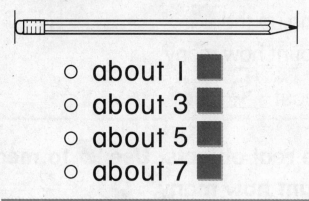

- ○ about 1 ▪
- ○ about 3 ▪
- ○ about 5 ▪
- ○ about 7 ▪

4. About how long is the eraser?

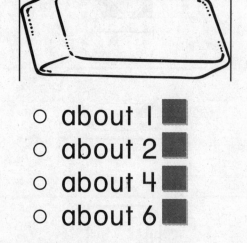

- ○ about 1 ▪
- ○ about 2 ▪
- ○ about 4 ▪
- ○ about 6 ▪

5. About how long is the string?

Draw ▪ to show your measure.   about _____ ▪

Name _____

Lesson 73

COMMON CORE STANDARD CC.1.MD.2
Lesson Objective: Make a nonstandard
measuring tool to measure length.

Make a Nonstandard Measuring Tool

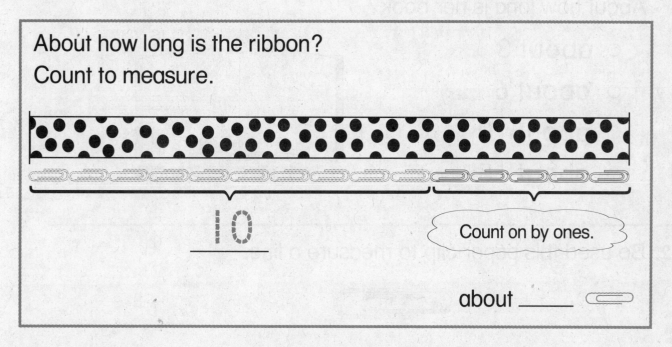

About how long is the ribbon?
Count to measure.

10

Count on by ones.

about _____

Use real objects and the measuring tool you made. Measure.

1.

about _____

2.

about _____

3.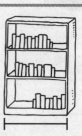

about _____

1. Joy measures her book with 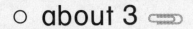 .
   About how long is her book?

   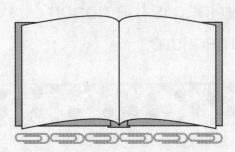

   ○ about 3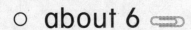

   ○ about 6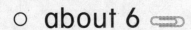

   ○ about 10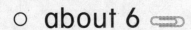

   ○ about 15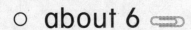

___

2. Bo used this paper clip to measure a line.

   Which line is about 3 paper clips long?

   ○ |————————————————|

   ○ |——————————————————————|

   ○ |—————————————————————————————|

   ○ |——————————|

___

3. Molly is measuring a paintbrush with paper clips.
   Write two things she should do.

   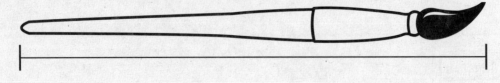

   _____

   _____

Name _____

Problem Solving •
Measure and Compare

The gray ribbon is 3 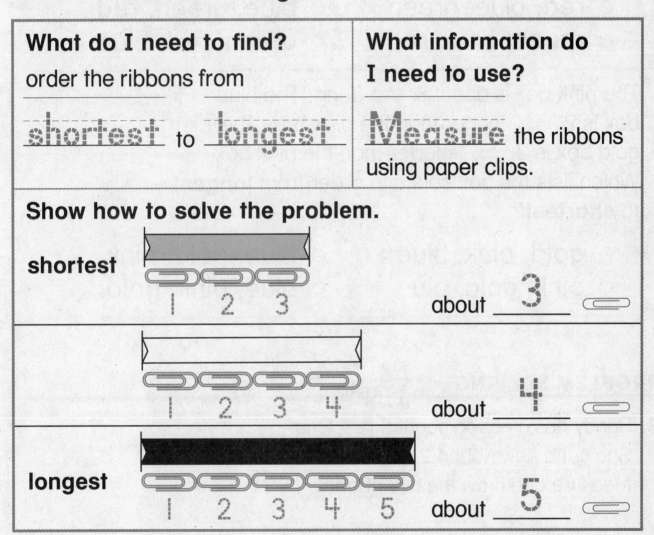 long. The white ribbon is
4 ⬭ long. The black ribbon is 1 ⬭ longer than the
white ribbon. Draw and color the length of the ribbons in
order from **shortest** to **longest**.

What do I need to find?	**What information do I need to use?**
order the ribbons from _____ _____	
<u>shortest</u> to <u>longest</u>	<u>Measure</u> the ribbons using paper clips.

Show how to solve the problem.

shortest
1 2 3   about ___3___ ⬭

1 2 3 4   about ___4___ ⬭

longest
1 2 3 4 5   about ___5___ ⬭

1. The _____ ribbon is the shortest ribbon.

2. The _____ ribbon is the longest ribbon.

1. The red book is about 9 ⊂⊃ long. The blue book is 2 ⊂⊃ shorter than the red book. The green book is 1 ⊂⊃ shorter than the blue book. Which lists the book colors in order from **shortest** to **longest**?

○ red, blue, green   ○ blue, green, red

○ green, blue, red   ○ green, red, blue

2. The pink box is about 8 ⊂⊃ long. The blue box is 2 ⊂⊃ longer than the pink box. The gold box is 3 ⊂⊃ shorter than the pink box. Which lists the box colors in order from **longest** to **shortest**?

○ gold, pink, blue   ○ blue, gold, pink

○ pink, gold, blue   ○ blue, pink, gold

PROBLEM SOLVING  REAL WORLD

3. Sandy has a ribbon about 4 ⊂⊃ long.
She cut a new ribbon 2 ⊂⊃ longer.
Measure and draw the two ribbons.

The new ribbon is about _____ ⊂⊃ long.

Name _____

Lesson 75

COMMON CORE STANDARD CC.1.MD.3
Lesson Objective: Write times to the hour shown on analog clocks.

Time to the Hour

Look at the hour hand.

The hour hand points to the __8__.

It is __8:00__.

Look at where the hour hand points.
Write the time.

1. The hour hand points to the _____.

It is _____.

2. The hour hand points to the _____.

It is _____.

3.

_____

4.

_____

5.

_____

1. Look at the hour hand.
   What is the time?

- ○ 5:00   ○ 3:00
- ○ 4:00   ○ 2:00

3. Look at the hour hand.
   What is the time?

- ○ 2:00   ○ 6:00
- ○ 5:00   ○ 12:00

2. Look at the hour hand.
   What is the time?

- ○ 11:00   ○ 8:00
- ○ 10:00   ○ 1:00

4. Look at the hour hand.
   What is the time?

- ○ 1:00   ○ 7:00
- ○ 6:00   ○ 8:00

5. Look at where the hour hand points.
   Write the time.

Name _____

Lesson 76

COMMON CORE STANDARD CC.1.MD.3

Lesson Objective: Write times to the half hour shown on analog clocks.

Time to the Half Hour

The hour hand points halfway between

the __9__ and the __10__.

It is __half past 9:00__.

Look at where the hour hand points.
Write the time.

1. The hour hand points halfway between

   the _____ and the _____.

   It is _____.

2. The hour hand points halfway between

   the _____ and the _____.

   It is _____.

3.

_____

4.

_____

5.

_____

Name _____

1. Look at the hour hand.
   What is the time?

○ 3:00
○ half past 3:00
○ 4:00
○ half past 4:00

2. Look at the hour hand.
   What is the time?

○ half past 5:00
○ 5:00
○ half past 4:00
○ 4:00

3. Look at the hour hand.
   What is the time?

○ half past 10:00
○ 10:00

○ half past 9:00
○ 9:00

4. Mindy woke up at 7:30. Leah ate lunch
   at 12:30. Write the name of the person
   whose activity matches the time.

_____

Name _____

Lesson 77

COMMON CORE STANDARD CC.1.MD.3

Lesson Objective: Tell times to the hour and half hour using analog and digital clocks.

Tell Time to the Hour and Half Hour

The short hand is the **hour hand**.
It shows the hour.

The long hand is the **minute hand**.
It shows the minutes after the hour.

There are 60 minutes
in one hour.

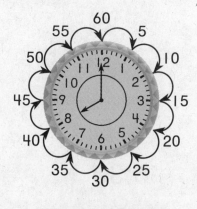

There are 30 minutes
in a half hour.

Write the time.

1.

2.

3.

Name _____

1. What time is shown on the clock?

5:30   5:00   4:30   3:00
 ○   ○   ○   ○

---

2. What time is it?

12:00   12:30   6:00   6:30
 ○   ○   ○   ○

---

3. Which clock shows 9:30?

   ○   ○   ○   ○

---

4. Write the time.

Lesson 78

COMMON CORE STANDARD CC.1.MD.3
Lesson Objective: Use the hour hand to draw
and write times on analog and digital clocks.

Practice Time to the
Hour and Half Hour

The hour hand points to 8.
The minute hand points
to 12.

8:00

The hour hand points between
8 and 9.
The minute hand points to 6.

8:30

Use the hour hand to write the time.
Draw the minute hand.

1.

_____

2.

_____

3.

_____

I. Which clock shows the correct time?

7:30

○   ○   ○   ○

---

2. Nora walked her dog for one hour. How many minutes did she walk her dog?

○   10 minutes
○   30 minutes
○   60 minutes
○   100 minutes

PROBLEM SOLVING REAL WORLD

Solve.

3. Billy played outside for a half hour.
Write how many minutes Billy
played outside.

_____ minutes

Name _____

Read Picture Graphs

Lesson 79

COMMON CORE STANDARD CC.1.MD.4

Lesson Objective: Analyze and compare data shown in a picture graph where each symbol represents one.

A **picture graph** uses pictures to show how many. Count the 🧍 in each row.

Snack We Like					
🍎 apple	🧍	🧍	🧍	🧍	🧍
🥨 pretzel	🧍	🧍	🧍		

Each 🧍 stands for 1 child who chose that snack.

There are __5__ children who chose 🍎.

There are __3__ children who chose 🥨.

Use the picture graph to answer each question.

What We Ate for Lunch							
🥪 sandwich	🧍	🧍	🧍	🧍	🧍	🧍	
🥫 soup	🧍	🧍					

Each 🧍 stands for 1 child.

1. Which lunch did more
   children choose? Circle.

2. How many children chose ? _____ children

3. How many children chose ? _____ children

Use the picture graph to answer the question.

Pets We Have							
🐕 dog	🧍	🧍	🧍	🧍	🧍	🧍	
🐈 cat	🧍	🧍	🧍	🧍	🧍		
🐹 hamster	🧍	🧍					

Each 🧍 stands for 1 child.

1. How many children in all have 🐈 and 🐹?

   ○ 3   ○ 7   ○ 4   ○ 11

2. How many children have ?

   ○ 2   ○ 4   ○ 5   ○ 6

3. How many more children have 🐕 than 🐈?

   ○ 11   ○ 6   ○ 5   ○ 1

4. How can you use the picture graph to find how many pets in all? Show your work.

   _____

   _____

Lesson 80

COMMON CORE STANDARD CC.1.MD.4

Lesson Objective: Make a picture graph where each symbol represents one and interpret the information.

Make Picture Graphs

Are there more black cars or white cars? Complete the picture graph to find out.

Cross out each car as you count.

Draw a ◯ in the graph to show each car.

Black and White Cars										
🚗 black	⟲									
🚗 white										

Each ◯ stands for 1 car.

Use the picture graph to answer each question.

1. How many 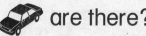 are there?   _____

2. How many 🚗 are there?   _____

3. Are there more  or 🚗? Circle.

Core Standards for Math, Grade 1

Name _____

Lesson 80
CC.1.MD.4

Use the picture graph to answer the question.

Our Favorite Zoo Animal									
ape	☺	☺	☺	☺	☺	☺	☺	☺	
lion	☺	☺	☺	☺	☺				
seal	☺	☺	☺	☺	☺	☺			

Each ☺ stands for 1 child.

1. How many children chose ?

   3   4   6   8
   ○   ○   ○   ○

2. Which animal did the fewest children choose?

                                 🦒
   ○   ○   ○   ○

3. Which animal did the most children choose?

   🦍   🦁   🦭   🦒
   ○   ○   ○   ○

4. How many more children chose 🦍 than 🦁 ?
   Show your work.

   _____

Name _____

Lesson 81

COMMON CORE STANDARD CC.1.MD.4
Lesson Objective: Analyze and compare data shown in a bar graph.

Read Bar Graphs

A **bar graph** uses a bar to show how many.

This graph shows 6 children chose .

The longest bar shows the snack most children chose.

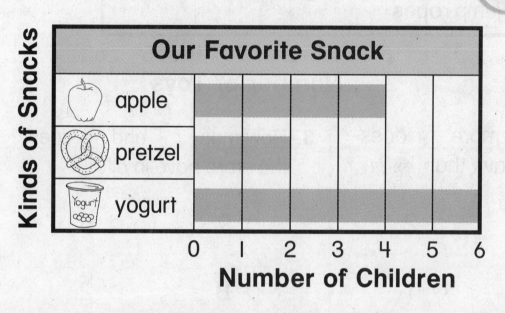

Kinds of Snacks

Our Favorite Snack

apple

pretzel

yogurt

0 1 2 3 4 5 6
Number of Children

Use the bar graph to answer the question.

1. How many children chose ? _____ children

2. How many children chose ? _____ children

3. Circle the snack the most children chose.

4. Circle the snack the fewest children chose.

Name ____________________

Lesson 81
CC.1.MD.4

Use the bar graph to answer the question.

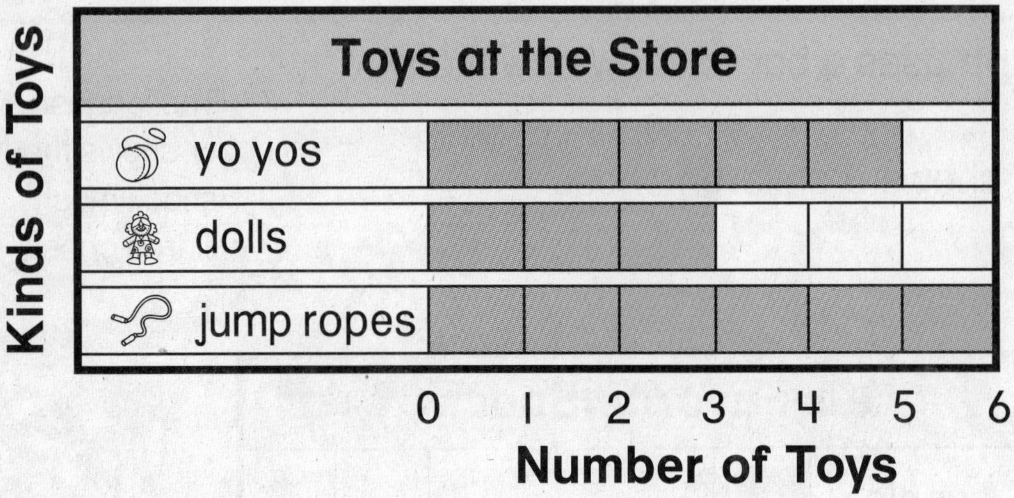

1. How many more yo yos does the store have than dolls?

○ 8 ○ 2

○ 3 ○ 1

2. How many jump ropes does the store have?

○ 2 ○ 5

○ 3 ○ 6

3. How many yo yos and dolls does the store have in all?

○ 9 ○ 5

○ 8 ○ 2

4. How many dolls does the store have?

○ 3 ○ 5

○ 4 ○ 6

5. How many yo yos were sold if the store started with 8? Show your work.

____

____

Make Bar Graphs

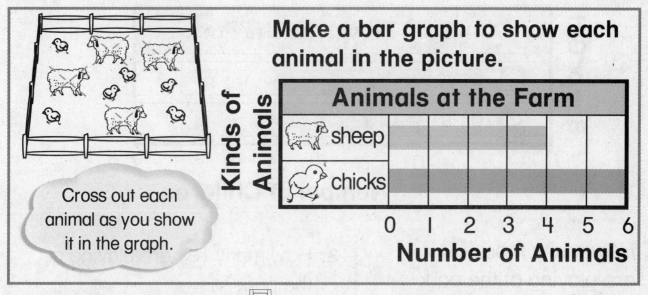

Make a bar graph to show each animal in the picture.

Cross out each animal as you show it in the graph.

Are there more or in your classroom?

1. Make a bar graph to find out.

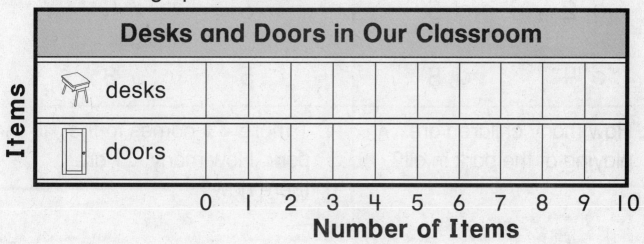

2. How many  are in your classroom?   _____

3. Are there more or
in your classroom? Circle.

Name _____

Use the bar graph to answer the question.

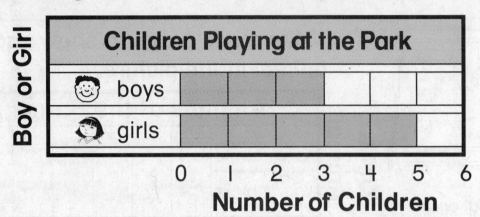

1. How many more are playing at the park than ?

  ○ 2   ○ 5

  ○ 4   ○ 8

3. How many are playing at the park?

  ○ 6   ○ 4

  ○ 5   ○ 3

2. How many children are playing at the park in all?

  ○ 8   ○ 5

  ○ 6   ○ 3

4. I more comes to the park. How many are there now?

  ○ 7   ○ 5

  ○ 6   ○ 4

5. 2 more come to the park.
Color the bar graph to show this.

Core Standards for Math, Grade 1

Name _____

Read Tally Charts

Lesson 83

COMMON CORE STANDARD CC.1.MD.4
Lesson Objective: Analyze and compare data shown in a tally chart.

Some children named their favorite collections.
Each | stands for 1 child.
Each ⅢⅠ stands for 5 children.

Our Favorite Thing to Collect			Total
🐚	shells	|||| 1 2 3 4	4
🚗	stamps	ⅢⅠ || 5 6 7	7

More children like to collect _____stamps_____.

Complete the tally chart.

Do you have a pet?		Total
yes	ⅢⅠ |||	
no	ⅢⅠ	

Use the tally chart to answer each question.

1. How many children have a pet? _____ children

2. How many children do not have a pet? _____ children

3. Did more children answer yes or no? _____

www.harcourtschoolsupply.com
© Houghton Mifflin Harcourt Publishing Company

165

Core Standards for Math, Grade 1

Use the tally chart to answer the question.

Our Favorite Lunch		Total
🍕 pizza |卌 |||	
🥪 sandwich	||||	
🍝 spaghetti	|||	

I. How many children chose 🥪?

2 ○   3 ○   4 ○   5 ○

2. How many more children chose 🥪 than 🍝?

1 ○   3 ○   4 ○   7 ○

3. How many children in all chose their favorite lunch?

16 ○   15 ○   12 ○   11 ○

4. Complete the tally chart. Write the numbers.

Name _____

Lesson 84

COMMON CORE STANDARD CC.1.MD.4

Lesson Objective: Make a tally chart and interpret the information.

Make Tally Charts

The picture shows shapes.
Make a tally chart to show
how many of each shape.

Cross out each
shape as you
count.

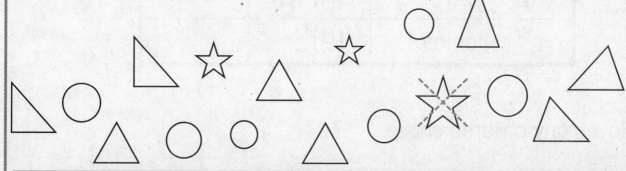

Shapes in the Picture		Total
◯ circles	⊬⊬1	6
☆ stars	|||	3
△ triangles	⊬⊬ |||	8

Use the tally chart to answer each question.

1. How many ☆ are there?

____ ☆

2. How many more △ than
   ◯ are there?

   ____ more △

3. Which shape is there
   the most of? Circle.

Core Standards for Math, Grade 1

Use the tally chart to answer the question.

Our Favorite Vegetable		Total
🥕 carrot	ⅢⅢ I	6
corn	ⅢⅢ IIII	9
🍅 tomato	ⅢⅢ	

1. How many children chose 🍅 ?

   2   5   6   9
   ○   ○   ○   ○

2. How many children chose corn and 🥕 ?

   6   9   14   15
   ○   ○   ○   ○

3. How many more children chose 🥕 than ?

   1   2   8   4
   ○   ○   ○   ○

4. How many children in all voted for a favorite vegetable? Show the total in tally marks. Then write the number.

_____ children in all.

Lesson 85

COMMON CORE STANDARD CC.1.MD.4
Lesson Objective: Solve problem
situations using the strategy *make a graph*.

Problem Solving • Represent Data

Ava has these beads to make a bracelet.
How can you find how many beads she has?

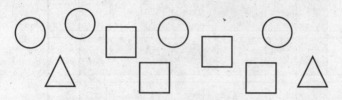

Unlock the Problem

What do I need to find? how many ___beads___ Ava has	**What information do I need to use?** the number of , _○_ , _△_ and _□_ in the picture

Show how to solve the problem.

> Color the first bar
> to show there are
> 4 circles.

Beads Ava Has						
circle ○						
square □						
triangle △						

0 1 2 3 4 5 6

Use the graph. Write how many. Add to solve.

1. _____**4**_____ ○ + ____ □ + ____ △ = ____

How many beads does Ava have? _____ beads

Core Standards for Math, Grade 1

Use the bar graph to answer the question.

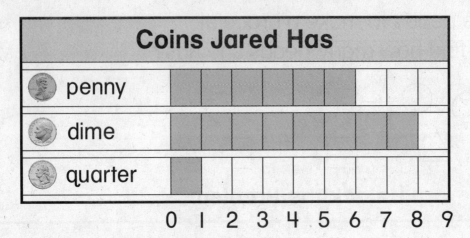

Coins Jared Has

1. How many fewer pennies than dimes does Jared have?

   ○ 1   ○ 2   ○ 3   ○ 4

2. How many dimes does Jared have?

   ○ 8   ○ 6   ○ 5   ○ 3

3. How many more dimes than quarters does Jared have?

   ○ 1   ○ 4   ○ 7   ○ 8

4. Look at the bar graph. Suppose Jared uses 3 dimes to buy a marker. How would the bar graph change?

   _____

   _____

Lesson 86

COMMON CORE STANDARD CC.1.G.1

Lesson Objective: Identify and describe three-dimensional shapes according to defining attributes.

Three-Dimensional Shapes

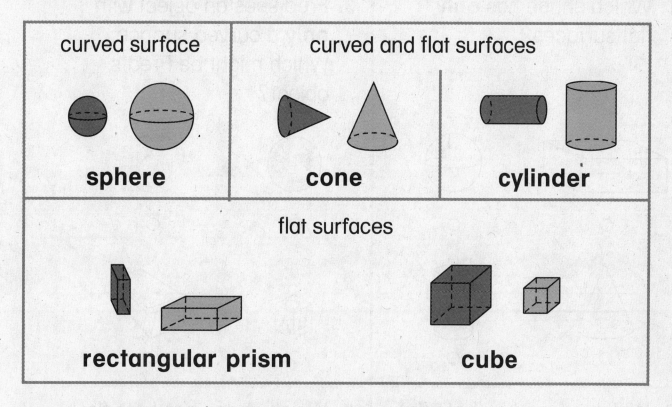

curved surface

sphere

curved and flat surfaces

cone

cylinder

flat surfaces

rectangular prism

cube

Color to sort the shapes into three groups.

1. only **flat surfaces** RED

2. only a **curved surface** BLUE

3. both **curved** and **flat surfaces** YELLOW

cone

cube

cylinder

sphere

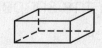

rectangular prism

1. Which shape has **only** flat surfaces?

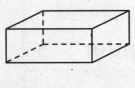 

○   ○

○   ○

3. Fred sees an object with **only** a curved surface. Which might be Fred's object?

○   ○

○   ○

2. Which shape has both flat and curved surfaces?

 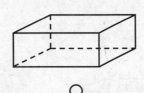

○   ○

○   ○

4. Which shape has both flat and curved surfaces?

 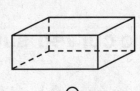

○   ○

 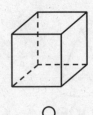

○   ○

5. Write the name of the shape.

_____

Name _____

Lesson 87

COMMON CORE STANDARD CC.1.G.1
Lesson Objective: Identify two-dimensional shapes on three-dimensional shapes.

Two-Dimensional Shapes on Three-Dimensional Shapes

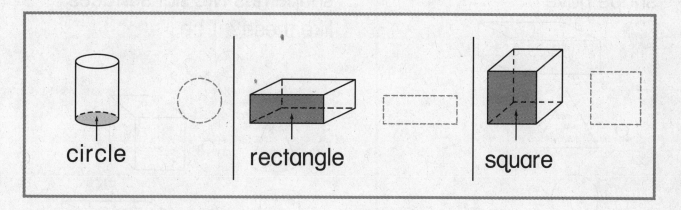

circle   rectangle   square

Look at the shape.
Circle the flat surfaces it has.

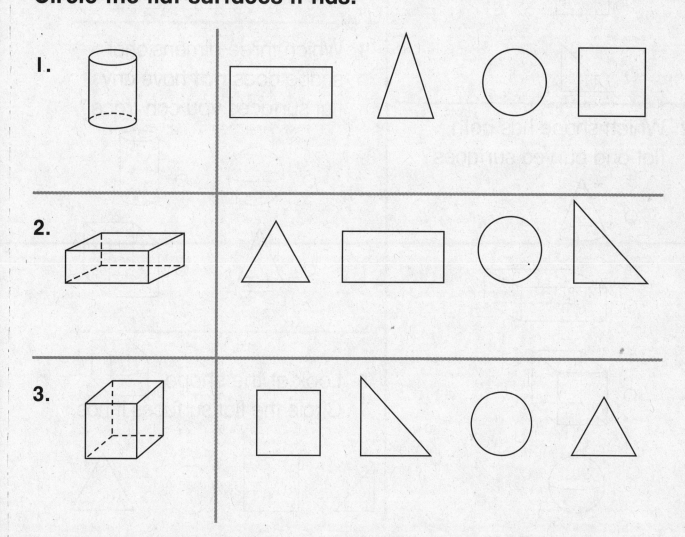

1.

2.

3.

1. Which flat surface does this shape have?

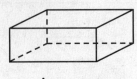

○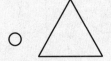

○

○

○

2. Which shape has both flat and curved surfaces?

○

○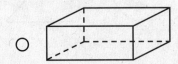

○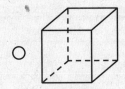

○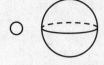

3. Which three-dimensional shape has two flat surfaces like these?

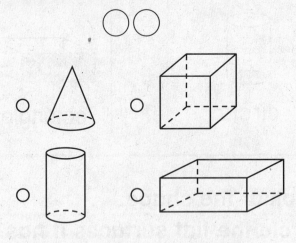

4. Which three-dimensional shape does **not** have any flat surfaces you can trace?

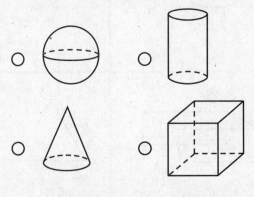

5. Look at the shape . Circle the flat surfaces it has.

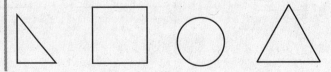

Core Standards for Math, Grade 1

Name _____

Lesson 88

COMMON CORE STANDARD CC.1.G.1
Lesson Objective: Use defining attributes to sort shapes.

Sort Two-Dimensional Shapes

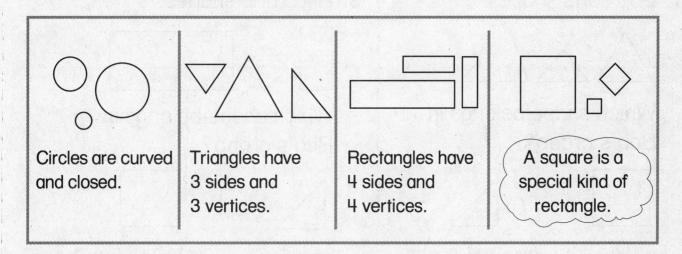

| Circles are curved and closed. | Triangles have 3 sides and 3 vertices. | Rectangles have 4 sides and 4 vertices. | A square is a special kind of rectangle. |

Read the sorting rule. Circle the shapes that follow the rule.

1. 4 sides

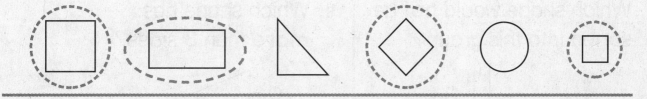

2. curved and closed

3. 3 vertices

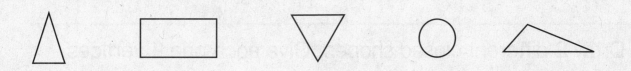

1. Bob sorts shapes.

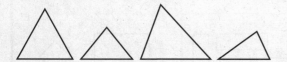

Which shape belongs in Bob's group?

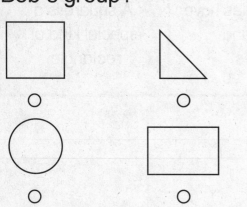

3. Rita sorts shapes.

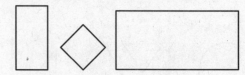

Which shape belongs in Rita's group?

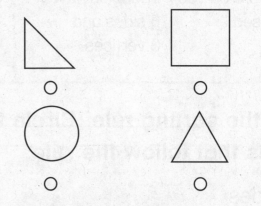

2. Which shape would **not** be sorted into this group?

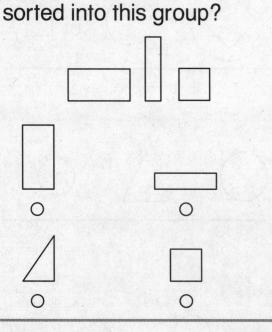

4. Which shape has **more** than 3 sides?

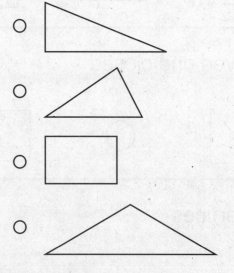

5. Draw 2 different closed shapes. Give each one 4 vertices.

Name _____

Lesson 89
COMMON CORE STANDARD CC.1.G.1
Lesson Objective: Describe attributes of two-dimensional shapes.

Describe Two-Dimensional Shapes

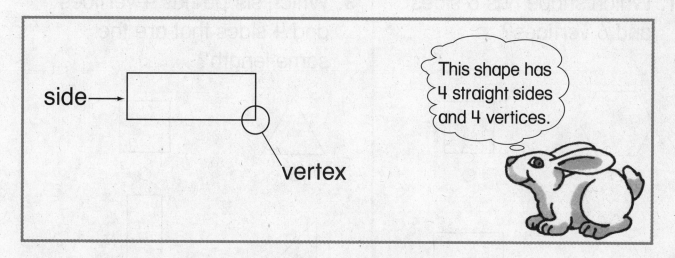

side →

vertex

This shape has 4 straight sides and 4 vertices.

Write the number of straight sides or vertices.

1. triangle

_3_ sides

2. square

____ vertices

3. hexagon

____ vertices

4. trapezoid

____ sides

5. triangle

____ vertices

6. square

____ sides

Name _____

1. Which shape has 6 sides and 6 vertices?

○   ○

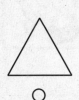

○   ○

3. Which shape has 4 vertices and 4 sides that are the same length?

○   ○

   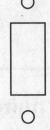

○   ○

2. How many straight sides does this shape have?

○ 1
○ 2
○ 3
○ 4

4. Which shape does **not** have 4 sides?

○   ○

   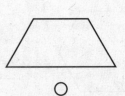

○   ○

5. Jed says that shapes cannot have curves.
Is he correct? Draw or write to explain.

Lesson 90

COMMON CORE STANDARD CC.1.G.2

Lesson Objective: Compose a new shape by combining three-dimensional shapes.

Combine Three-Dimensional Shapes

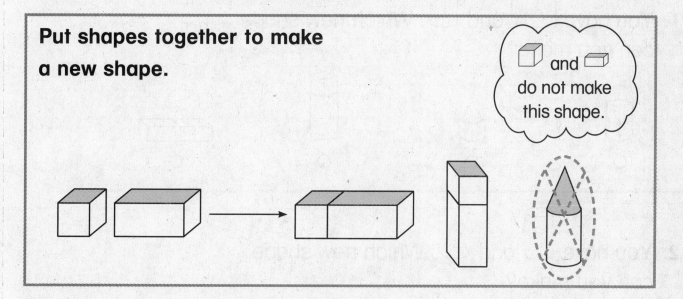

Put shapes together to make a new shape.

and do not make this shape.

Use three-dimensional shapes.

Combine.	Which new shapes can you make? Circle them.
1.	
2.	

1. You have and . Which new shape can you make?

 ○    ○    ○   ○

2. You have and . Which new shape can you make?

 ○   ○   ○   ○

3. You have two . Which new shape can you make?

 ○   ○   ○   ○

4. Circle the shape that **cannot** be made from .

Name _____

Lesson 91

COMMON CORE STANDARD CC.1.G.2
Lesson Objective: Use composite
three-dimensional shapes to build new
shapes.

Make New Three-Dimensional Shapes

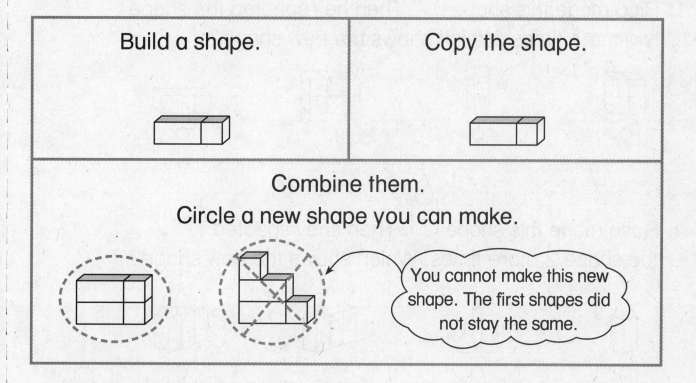

Build a shape.

Copy the shape.

Combine them.
Circle a new shape you can make.

You cannot make this new shape. The first shapes did not stay the same.

Use three-dimensional shapes.

Build these shapes.	Circle the new shape you can make. Cross out the shape you cannot make.
1.	
2.	

Name _____

1. Rico made this shape . Then he repeated the shape two more times. Which shows the new shape?

   ○   ○   ○   ○

2. Rosa made this shape . Then she repeated the shape 2 more times. Which shows the new shape?

   ○   ○   ○   ○

3. Remy made the shape 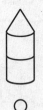. Then he repeated the shape. Which shows the new shape?

   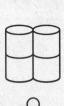
   ○   ○   ○   ○

PROBLEM SOLVING REAL WORLD

4. Dave builds this shape.
   Then he repeats and combines.
   Draw a shape he can make.

Core Standards for Math, Grade 1

Name _____

Lesson 92

COMMON CORE STANDARD CC.1.G.2

Lesson Objective: Identify three-dimensional shapes used to build a composite shape using the strategy *act it out*.

Problem Solving • Take Apart Three-Dimensional Shapes

Kate has △, ▢, ◻, and ▢.
She built a tower.
Which shapes did Kate
use to build the tower?

Unlock the Problem

What do I need to find?	**What information do I need to use?**
which <u>shapes</u> Kate used to build the tower	Kate has these shapes.

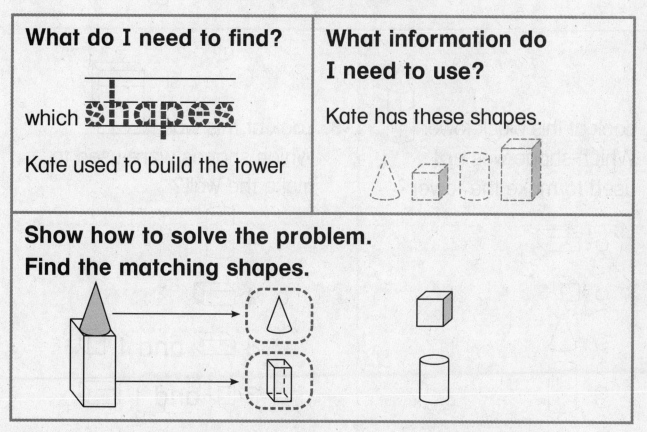

Show how to solve the problem.
Find the matching shapes.

Use three-dimensional shapes. Circle your answer.

1. Which shapes did Marvin use to build this bench?

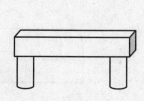

1. Which shapes did Jody use to make this tower?

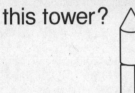

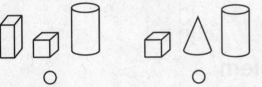

○   ○   ○   ○

2. Look at this block tower . Which shape was **not** used to make the tower?

○   (rectangular prism)

○   (cube)

○   (cone)

○   (cylinder)

3. Look at this wall 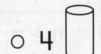. Which shapes were used to make the wall?

○ 4 (cylinder)

○ 4 (rectangular prism)

○ 3 (rectangular prism) and 1 (cube)

○ 3 (cube) and 1 (rectangular prism)

PROBLEM SOLVING REAL WORLD

4. Circle the ways that show the same shape.

         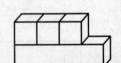

Lesson 93

COMMON CORE STANDARD CC.1.G.2
Lesson Objective: Use objects to compose new two-dimensional shapes.

Combine Two-Dimensional Shapes

You can put shapes together to make
a new shape.

3 _____ △ make
a ⬡.

Use pattern blocks. Draw to show the blocks.
Write how many blocks you used.

1. How many ⬡ make a ⬡ ?

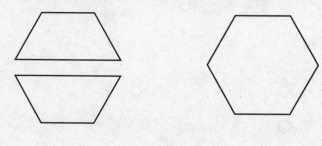

_____ ⬡ make a ⬡.

2. How many ◇ make a ⬡ ?

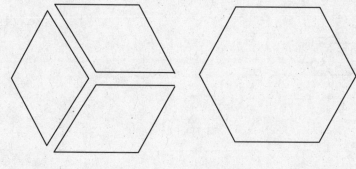

_____ ◇ make a ⬡.

Core Standards for Math, Grade 1

Use pattern blocks.

1. How many △ make a ◇?

   1   2   3   4
   ○   ○   ○   ○

_____

2. How many ◇ make a ⬡?

   9   6   3   2
   ○   ○   ○   ○

_____

3. How many ⬠ make 2 ⬡?

   2   4   6   8
   ○   ○   ○   ○

PROBLEM SOLVING REAL WORLD

Use pattern blocks. Draw to show your answer.

4. 2 ⬠ make a ⬡.

   How many ⬠ make 4 ⬡?

   ____ ⬠ make 4 ⬡.

Name _____

Lesson 94
COMMON CORE STANDARD CC.1.G.2
Lesson Objective: Compose a new shape
by combining two-dimensional shapes.

Combine More Shapes

Combine shapes to make a new shape.

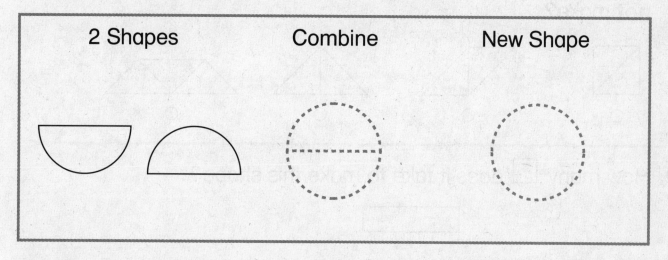

2 Shapes	Combine	New Shape

Circle the shapes that can combine to make the new shape.

I.

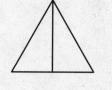

2.

3.

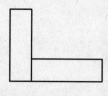

Core Standards for Math, Grade 1

1. Guy has 2 . Which shape can he **not** make?

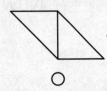   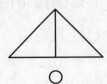   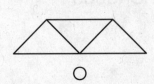

○   ○   ○   ○

---

2. How many  does it take to make this shape?

○

2   3   4   6
○   ○   ○   ○

---

3. Which shapes can combine to make this new shape?

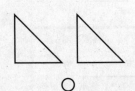   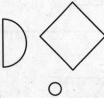   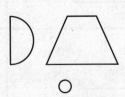

○   ○   ○   ○

---

4. Draw a new shape you can make from these shapes.

Name _____

Lesson 95

COMMON CORE STANDARD CC.1.G.2

Lesson Objective: Make new shapes from composite two-dimensional shapes using the strategy *act it out*.

Problem Solving • Make New Two-Dimensional Shapes

Luis wants to use △ to make a ◇.
How many △ does he need?

Unlock the Problem

What do I need to find?	**What information do I need to use?**
how Luis can make a ◇ _____ using △ _____	Luis uses △

Show how to solve the problem.

_2_ △ make a ◇.

Use shapes to solve.

1. Meg wants to use △
   to make a ▱.

   _____ △ make a ▱.

1. How many does it take to make one circle?

2   4   5   6

2. How many does it take to make **two** circles?

8   6   4   2

3. Rico combines 2 of the same shape to make a hexagon. Which shape did he use?

4. Draw a new shape made with 1  and 2 . Describe your shape.

_____

Name _____

Lesson 96
COMMON CORE STANDARD CC.1.G.2
Lesson Objective: Decompose combined shapes into shapes.

Find Shapes in Shapes

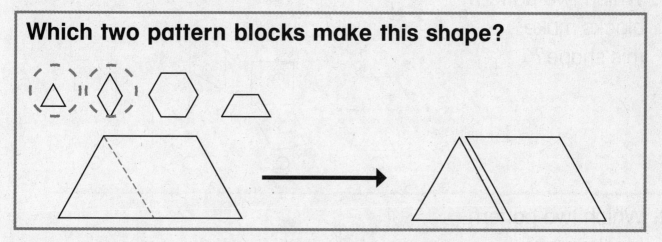

Which two pattern blocks make this shape?

Use two pattern blocks to make the shape.
Circle the blocks you use.

1.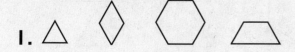

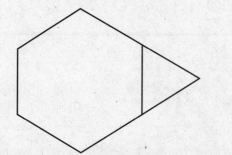

2.

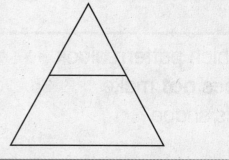

3.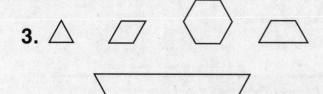

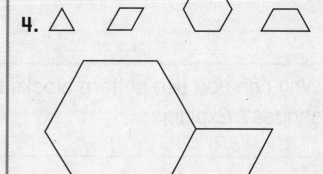

4.

1. Which two pattern
   blocks make
   this shape?

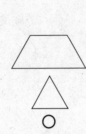 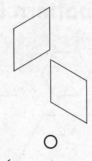 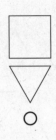

2. Which two pattern
   blocks make
   this shape?

 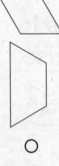 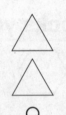 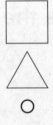

3. Which pattern block
   does **not** make
   this shape?

4. Why can you use pattern blocks to make new
   shapes? Explain.

_____

_____

_____

_____

Take Apart Two-Dimensional Shapes

Use pattern blocks to help you find the parts of a shape.

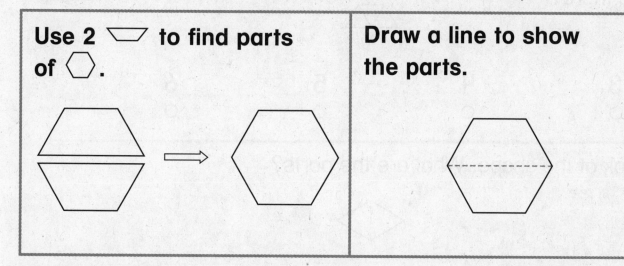

Use 2 ▽ to find parts of ⬡.

Draw a line to show the parts.

Use pattern blocks. Draw a line to show the parts.

1. Show 2 △.

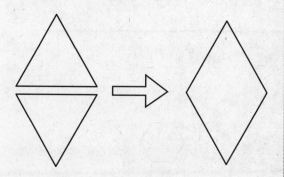

2. Show 2 ▽.

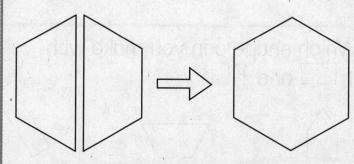

3. Show 2 □.

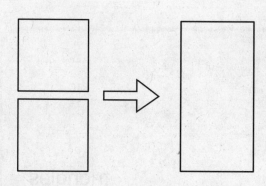

4. Show 2 ◠.

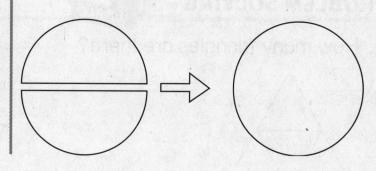

1. Look at the shape. How many triangles are there?

3   4   5   6
○   ○   ○   ○

2. Look at the shape. What are the parts?

○   ○   ○   ○

3. Which shape can you make with
1 ▭ and 1 □ ?

○   ○   ○   ○

PROBLEM SOLVING REAL WORLD

4. How many triangles are there?

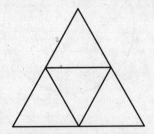

_____ triangles

COMMON CORE STANDARD CC.1.G.3
Lesson Objective: Identify equal and unequal parts (or shares) in two-dimensional shapes.

Equal or Unequal Parts

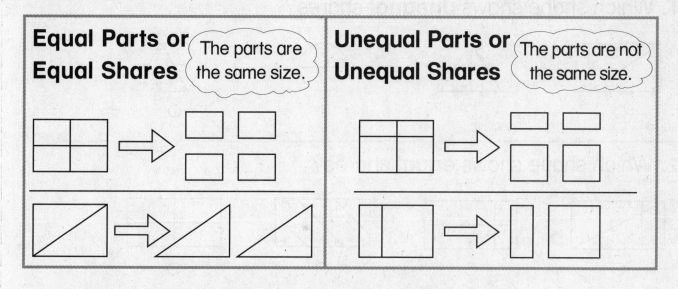

Equal Parts or Equal Shares — The parts are the same size.

Unequal Parts or Unequal Shares — The parts are not the same size.

Circle the shapes that show equal parts.
Cross out the shapes that show unequal parts.

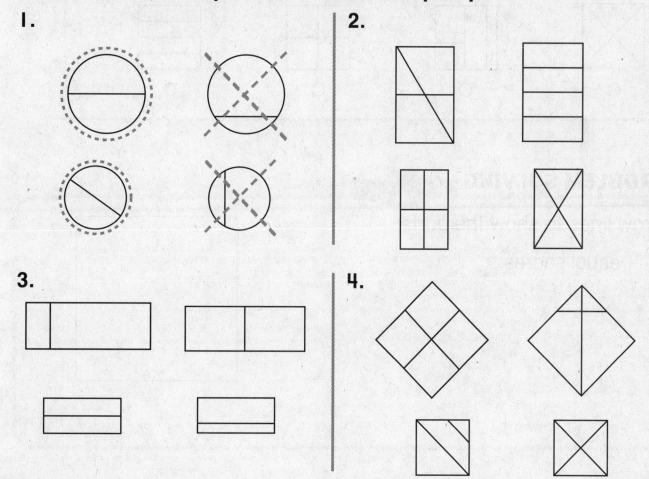

1.

2.

3.

4.

Core Standards for Math, Grade 1

1. Which shape shows **unequal** shares?

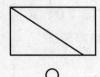

○   ○   ○   ○

2. Which shape shows **equal** shares?

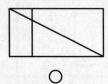 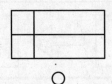 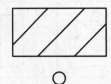 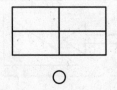

○   ○   ○   ○

3. Which shape shows 4 **unequal** shares?

  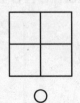 

○   ○   ○   ○

PROBLEM SOLVING REAL WORLD

Draw lines to show the parts.

4. 4 equal shares

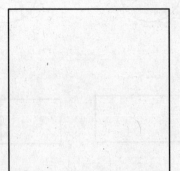

Name _____

Lesson 99

COMMON CORE STANDARD CC.1.G.3
Lesson Objective: Partition circles and rectangles into two equal shares.

Halves

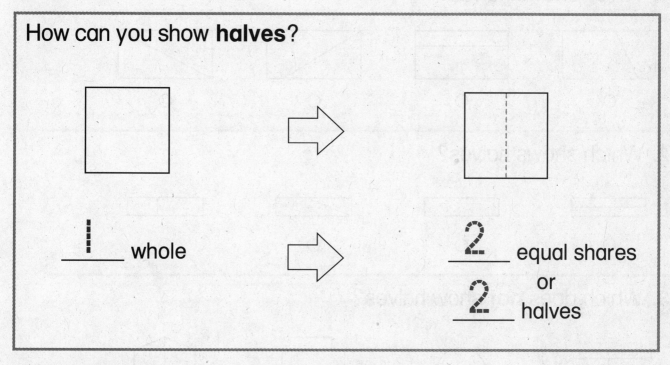

How can you show **halves**?

___1___ whole   ➡   ___2___ equal shares
or
___2___ halves

Draw a line to show halves. Write the numbers.

1.

_____ whole   _____ halves

2.

_____ whole   _____ halves

1. Which shows halves?

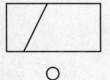 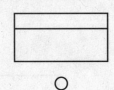 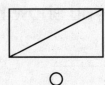 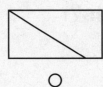

◯   ◯   ◯   ◯

2. Which shows halves?

◯   ◯   ◯   ◯

3. Which does **not** show halves?

  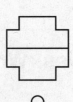 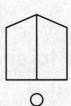

◯   ◯   ◯   ◯

PROBLEM SOLVING

Draw or write to solve.

4. Kate cut a square into equal shares. She traced one of the parts. Write **half of** or **halves** to name the part.

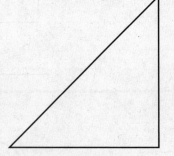

_____

_ _ _ _ _ _ _ _ _ _ _

_____ a square

Name _____

Lesson 100

COMMON CORE STANDARD CC.1.G.3

Lesson Objective: Partition circles and rectangles into four equal shares.

Fourths

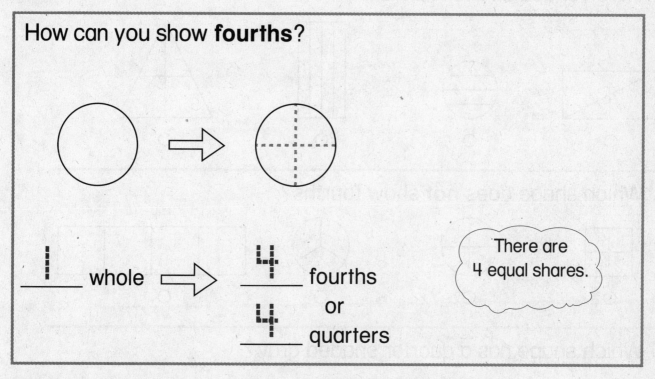

How can you show **fourths**?

_____ whole ⟹ __4__ fourths

or

__4__ quarters

There are 4 equal shares.

Draw lines to show fourths. Write the number.

1.

_____ whole   _____ fourths

2. Draw lines to show quarters. Write the number.

_____ whole   _____ fourths

Core Standards for Math, Grade 1

1. Which shape shows fourths?

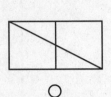   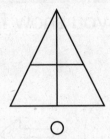

○   ○   ○   ○

2. Which shape does **not** show fourths?

   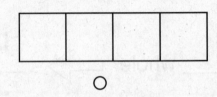

○   ○   ○   ○

3. Which shape has a quarter shaded gray?

 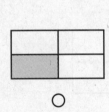 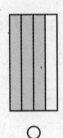

○   ○   ○   ○

PROBLEM SOLVING

Solve.

4. Chad drew a picture to show a
   quarter of a circle. Which shape
   did Chad draw? Circle it.

Answer Key

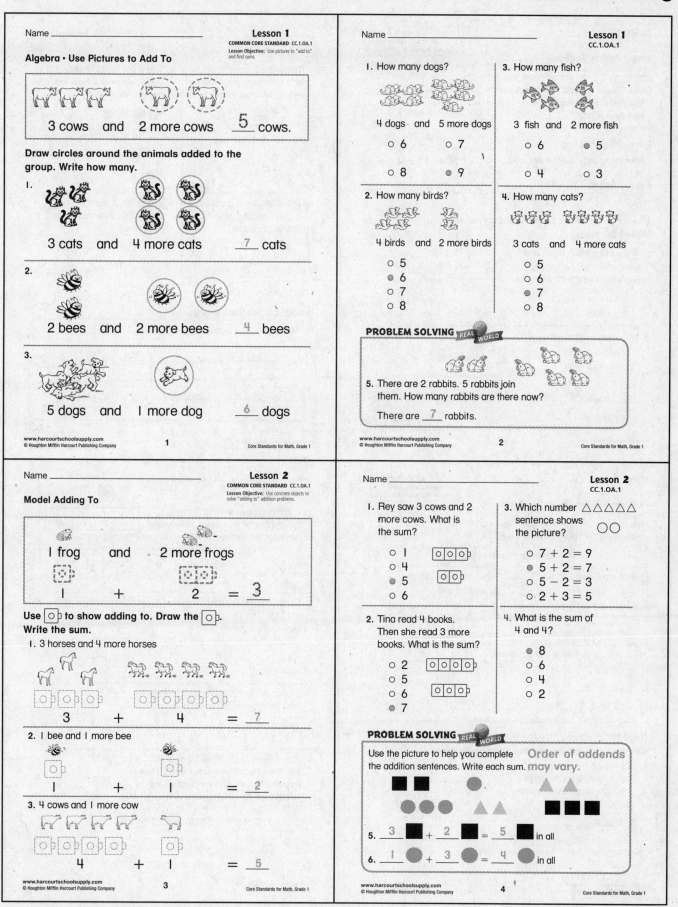

Lesson 1

COMMON CORE STANDARD CC.1.OA.1
Lesson Objective: Use pictures to "add to" and find sums.

Algebra • Use Pictures to Add To

3 cows   and   2 more cows   __5__ cows.

Draw circles around the animals added to the group. Write how many.

1. 3 cats   and   4 more cats   __7__ cats

2. 2 bees   and   2 more bees   __4__ bees

3. 5 dogs   and   1 more dog   __6__ dogs

www.harcourtschoolsupply.com
© Houghton Mifflin Harcourt Publishing Company

1

Core Standards for Math, Grade 1

Lesson 1
CC.1.OA.1

1. How many dogs?

   4 dogs   and   5 more dogs

   ○ 6   ○ 7
   ○ 8   ● 9

2. How many birds?

   4 birds   and   2 more birds

   ○ 5
   ● 6
   ○ 7
   ○ 8

3. How many fish?

   3 fish   and   2 more fish

   ○ 6   ● 5
   ○ 4   ○ 3

4. How many cats?

   3 cats   and   4 more cats

   ○ 5
   ○ 6
   ● 7
   ○ 8

PROBLEM SOLVING REAL WORLD

5. There are 2 rabbits. 5 rabbits join them. How many rabbits are there now?

   There are __7__ rabbits.

www.harcourtschoolsupply.com
© Houghton Mifflin Harcourt Publishing Company

2

Core Standards for Math, Grade 1

Lesson 2

COMMON CORE STANDARD CC.1.OA.1
Lesson Objective: Use concrete objects to solve "adding to" addition problems.

Model Adding To

1 frog   and   2 more frogs

1   +   2   =   3

Use ☐ to show adding to. Draw the ☐.
Write the sum.

1. 3 horses and 4 more horses

   3   +   4   =   __7__

2. 1 bee and 1 more bee

   1   +   1   =   __2__

3. 4 cows and 1 more cow

   4   +   1   =   __5__

www.harcourtschoolsupply.com
© Houghton Mifflin Harcourt Publishing Company

3

Core Standards for Math, Grade 1

Lesson 2
CC.1.OA.1

1. Rey saw 3 cows and 2 more cows. What is the sum?

   ○ 1
   ○ 4
   ● 5
   ○ 6

2. Tina read 4 books. Then she read 3 more books. What is the sum?

   ○ 2
   ○ 5
   ○ 6
   ● 7

3. Which number sentence shows the picture? △△△△△ ○○

   ○ 7 + 2 = 9
   ● 5 + 2 = 7
   ○ 5 − 2 = 3
   ○ 2 + 3 = 5

4. What is the sum of 4 and 4?

   ● 8
   ○ 6
   ○ 4
   ○ 2

PROBLEM SOLVING REAL WORLD

Use the picture to help you complete the addition sentences. Write each sum. *Order of addends may vary.*

5. __3__ + __2__ = __5__ in all

6. __1__ + __3__ = __4__ in all

www.harcourtschoolsupply.com
© Houghton Mifflin Harcourt Publishing Company

4

Core Standards for Math, Grade 1

Answer Key

Name _____

Lesson 3
COMMON CORE STANDARD CC.1.OA.1
Lesson Objective: Use concrete objects to solve "putting together" addition problems.

Model Putting Together

Use ⬤ ⭕ to add two groups.
Put the groups together to find how many.
There are 3 brown dogs.
There is 1 white dog.
How many dogs are there?

$3 + 1 = 4$

__4__ dogs

Use ⬤ ⭕ to solve. Draw to show your work.
Write how many.

1. There are 4 black bears and 3 brown bears. How many bears are there?

   __7__ bears $4 + 3 = \underline{7}$

2. There are 6 red flowers and 2 white flowers. How many flowers are there?

   __8__ flowers $6 + 2 = \underline{8}$

Name _____

Lesson 3
CC.1.OA.1

1. There are 2 large flowers and 1 small flower. How many flowers are there?

   ⬤⬤ ⭕

   $2 + 1 = \underline{}$
   - ○ 4   ● 3
   - ○ 2   ○ 1

3. There are 4 red flowers and 2 yellow flowers. How many flowers are there?

   ⬤⬤⬤⬤ ⭕⭕

   $4 + 2 = \underline{}$
   - ○ 3   ○ 5
   - ● 6   ○ 7

2. There are 3 red grapes and 6 green grapes. How many grapes are there?
   - ● 9   ○ 8
   - ○ 7   ○ 6

4. There are 3 black fish and 2 blue fish. How many fish are there?
   - ○ 1   ○ 3
   - ○ 4   ● 5

PROBLEM SOLVING REAL WORLD

5. Write your own addition story problem.

   Possible answer: There are 2 big cats and
   2 small cats. How many cats are there?

Name _____

Lesson 4
COMMON CORE STANDARD CC.1.OA.1
Lesson Objective: Solve adding to and putting together situations using the strategy make a model.

Problem Solving · Model Addition

Rico has 3 ✏️. Then he gets 1 more ✏️. How many ✏️ does he have now?

Unlock the Problem

What do I need to find?	What information do I need to use?
the number of _crayons_ Rico has now	Rico has _3_ ✏️ He gets _1_ ✏️

Show how to solve the problem.

3	1

$3 + 1 = \underline{4}$ __4__

Read the problem. Use the bar model to solve.
Complete the model and the number sentence.

1. There are 5 birds flying. Then 3 more birds join them. How many birds are flying now?

5	3

   $5 + 3 = \underline{8}$ __8__

Name _____

Lesson 4
CC.1.OA.1

1. 7 ladybugs are walking. 3 more ladybugs walk with them. How many ladybugs are walking now?

7	3

   10   7   4   3
   ●   ○   ○   ○

2. Marco has 10 toy cars. 6 cars are blue. The rest are silver. How many cars are silver?

6	___
   10

   16   10   6   4
   ○   ○   ○   ●

3. 6 bees are in a hive. 3 more bees fly in. How many bees are in the hive now?

   9   8   7   3
   ●   ○   ○   ○

4. There are 4 birds. Then other birds join them. Now there are 7 birds. How many birds joined them? Draw a model to solve. Write a number sentence.

   Check children's models; $4 + 3 = 7$

Lesson 5

Name _____

COMMON CORE STANDARD CC.1.OA.1
Lesson Objective: Model and record all the ways to put together numbers within 10.

Algebra • Put Together
Numbers to 10

You can use ⬤ to model ways to make 7.

○○○○○○⬤ $6 + \underline{1} = 7$

○○○○○⬤⬤ $5 + \underline{2} = 7$

Use ⬤. **Draw to show how to make 7.**
Complete the addition sentences.

1. ○○○○○○○ $4 + \underline{3} = 7$

2. ○○○○○○○ $3 + \underline{4} = 7$

3. ○○○○○○○ $2 + \underline{5} = 7$

4. ○○○○○○○ $1 + \underline{6} = 7$

Lesson 5
CC.1.OA.1

Name _____

1. Which shows a way to make 5?
   - ○
   - ⬤
   - ○
   - ○

2. Which shows a way to make 8?
   - ○
   - ○
   - ⬤
   - ○

3. Which is **not** a way to make 10?
   - ⬤ 0 + 1
   - ○ 3 + 7
   - ○ 5 + 5
   - ○ 8 + 2

4. Which is **not** a way to make 9?
   - ○ 8 + 1
   - ○ 7 + 2
   - ○ 6 + 3
   - ⬤ 5 + 5

5. Color ▢ to show a way to make 6. Write two addition sentences to go with your picture.

   ○○○○○○

   Check children's drawings. Possible answer:
   $2 + 4 = 6, \ 4 + 2 = 6$

Lesson 6

Name _____

COMMON CORE STANDARD CC.1.OA.1
Lesson Objective: Use pictures to show "taking from" and find differences.

Use Pictures to Show Taking From

Use the picture.

5 rabbits   3 hop away. $\underline{2}$ rabbits now

Write how many there are now.

1.

8 birds   4 fly away. $\underline{4}$ birds now

2.

7 bees   2 fly away. $\underline{5}$ bees now

Lesson 6
CC.1.OA.1

Name _____

1. There are 8 frogs. 2 frogs hop away. How many frogs are there now?
   - ○ 2
   - ⬤ 6
   - ○ 8
   - ○ 10

2. There are 7 cats. 3 cats run away. How many cats are there now?
   - ⬤ 4
   - ○ 7
   - ○ 10
   - ○ 11

3. There are 6 dogs. 3 dogs walk away. How many dogs are there now?
   - ○ 9
   - ○ 6
   - ⬤ 3
   - ○ 1

4. There are 5 fish. 4 fish swim away. How many fish are there now?
   - ○ 9
   - ○ 3
   - ○ 2
   - ⬤ 1

PROBLEM SOLVING REAL WORLD

Solve.

5. There are 7 birds. 2 birds fly away. How many birds are there now?

   $\underline{5}$ birds

Answer Key

Name _____ **Lesson 7**
COMMON CORE STANDARD CC.1.OA.1
Lesson Objective: Use concrete objects to solve "taking from" subtraction problems.

Model Taking From

Circle the part you take from the group.
Then cross it out.

3 dogs   2 dogs run away. | 1 dog now

$$3 - 2 = \underline{1}$$

Circle the part you take from the group.
Then cross it out. Write the difference.

1. 4 goats   2 goats walk away.   <u>2</u> goats now

$$4 - 2 = \underline{2}$$

2. 6 ants   3 ants walk away.   <u>3</u> ants now

$$6 - 3 = \underline{3}$$

www.harcourtschoolsupply.com
© Houghton Mifflin Harcourt Publishing Company   13   Core Standards for Math, Grade 1

Name _____ **Lesson 7**
CC.1.OA.1

1. What is the difference?

$$7 - 3 = \underline{}$$

- ○ 3
- ● 4
- ○ 7
- ○ 10

2. What is the difference?

$$10 - 8 = \underline{}$$

- ● 2
- ○ 7
- ○ 9
- ○ 16

3. What is the difference?

- ○ 7
- ○ 5
- ● 3
- ○ 2

4. What is the difference?

- ○ 2
- ● 5
- ○ 10
- ○ 15

PROBLEM SOLVING REAL WORLD

Draw ⚁ to solve. Complete the subtraction sentence.

Check children's drawings.

5. There are 8 fish.
4 fish swim away.
How many fish are there now?

$$\underline{8} - \underline{4} = \underline{4}$$
$$\underline{4} \text{ fish}$$

www.harcourtschoolsupply.com
© Houghton Mifflin Harcourt Publishing Company   14   Core Standards for Math, Grade 1

Name _____ **Lesson 8**
COMMON CORE STANDARD CC.1.OA.1
Lesson Objective: Use concrete objects to solve "taking apart" subtraction problems.

Model Taking Apart

You can use ○ to **subtract**.
Sam has 6 cars. 4 cars are red.
The rest are yellow.
How many cars are yellow?

<u>2</u> cars are yellow.   ●●●●○○

$$\underline{6} - \underline{4} = \underline{2}$$

Use ○ to solve. Color. Write the number sentence and how many.

1. There are 5 books.
1 book is red. The rest are yellow. How many books are yellow?

 R Y Y Y Y

$$\underline{5} \ominus \underline{1} = \underline{4}$$

<u>4</u> yellow books

2. There are 6 blocks.
3 blocks are small.
The rest are big.
How many blocks are big?

R R R Y Y Y

$$\underline{6} \ominus \underline{3} = \underline{3}$$

<u>3</u> big blocks

www.harcourtschoolsupply.com
© Houghton Mifflin Harcourt Publishing Company   15   Core Standards for Math, Grade 1

Name _____ **Lesson 8**
CC.1.OA.1

1. There are 6 snakes.
2 snakes are green. The rest are brown. How many snakes are brown?

- ○ $6 - 4 = 2$
- ● $6 - 2 = 4$
- ○ $2 + 4 = 6$
- ○ $6 + 2 = 8$

2. There are 7 tents. 3 tents are blue. The rest are orange. How many tents are orange?

- ○ $7 + 3 = 10$
- ○ $4 + 3 = 7$
- ● $7 - 3 = 4$
- ○ $7 - 4 = 3$

3. There are 5 snails. 4 snails are small. The rest are big. How many snails are big?

- ○ 3
- ○ 2
- ● 1
- ○ 0

4. There are 8 trees. 3 trees are pines. The rest are oaks. How many trees are oaks?

- ● 5
- ○ 4
- ○ 3
- ○ 2

PROBLEM SOLVING REAL WORLD

Solve. Draw a model to explain.

Check children's drawings.

5. There are 8 cats. 6 cats walk away. How many cats are left?

<u>2</u> cats left

www.harcourtschoolsupply.com
© Houghton Mifflin Harcourt Publishing Company   16   Core Standards for Math, Grade 1

Answer Key

Name _____

Lesson 9
COMMON CORE STANDARD CC.1.OA.1
Lesson Objective: Solve taking from and taking apart subtraction problems using the strategy *make a model*.

Problem Solving • Model Subtraction

There were 9 bugs on a rock. 7 bugs ran away.
How many bugs are on the rock now?

What do I need to find?	What information do I need to use?
how many __bugs__ on the rock now	__9__ bugs on a rock __7__ bugs ran away

Show how to solve the problem.

7	2
9	

$9 - 7 = 2$

Read the problem. Use the model to solve.
Complete the model and the number sentence.

1. There are 5 birds. 1 bird is big. The rest are small.
   How many birds are small?

1	4
5	

$5 - 1 = 4$

Name _____

Lesson 9
CC.1.OA.1

1. A shop had some fish in a tank. 4 fish were sold. Then there were 5 fish left in the tank. How many fish did the shop have?
   - ○ 1
   - ○ 3
   - ○ 8
   - ● 9

3. Kenny has 7 pets. 3 are turtles. The rest are birds. How many birds does Kenny have?
   - ○ 10
   - ○ 5
   - ● 4
   - ○ 3

2. There are 10 hats. 4 hats are blue. The rest are red. How many hats are red?
   - ○ 10
   - ● 6
   - ○ 5
   - ○ 4

4. There were 9 girls at the party. Some girls left. Then there were 3 girls. How many girls left?
   - ● 6
   - ○ 5
   - ○ 4
   - ○ 3

5. Nell has 7 books. 5 are picture books. The rest are chapter books. How many chapter books does Nell have? Complete the model and number sentence.

5	2
7	

$7 \, (-) \, 5 \, (=) \, 2$

Name _____

Lesson 10
COMMON CORE STANDARD CC.1.OA.1
Lesson Objective: Model and compare groups to show the meaning of subtraction.

Subtract to Compare

You can use ▦ to show the bar model.

8 ●●●●●●●●
6 ○○○○○○

Andy has 8 balloons.
Jill has 6 balloons.
How many more balloons does Andy have than Jill?

8	
6	2

__2__ more balloons

$8 - 6 = 2$

Read the problem. Use the bar model to solve. Write the number sentence. Then write how many.

1. Bo has 6 rocks.
   Jen has 4 rocks.
   How many more rocks does Bo have than Jen?

6 ●●●●●●
4 ○○○○

6	
4	2

__2__ more rocks

$6 - 4 = 2$

Name _____

Lesson 10
CC.1.OA.1

1. Eli has 5 pens. Hana has 8 pens. How many fewer pens does Eli have?

8
5

   - 2 ○
   - 3 ●
   - 4 ○
   - 5 ○

2. Kim has 4 shells. Josh has 6 shells. How many more shells does Josh have than Kim?

6
4

   - 10 ○
   - 5 ○
   - 3 ○
   - 2 ●

3. Erin has 4 pennies. Ryan has 10 pennies. How many fewer pennies does Erin have than Ryan?

10
4

   - 6 ●
   - 5 ○
   - 4 ○
   - 3 ○

PROBLEM SOLVING REAL WORLD

Complete the number sentence to solve.

4. Maya has 7 pens. Sam has 1 pen. How many more pens does Maya have than Sam?

$7 - 1 = 6$

__6__ more pens

Answer Key

Lesson 11
COMMON CORE STANDARD CC.1.OA.1
Lesson Objective: Model and record all of the ways to take apart numbers within 10.

Name _____

Algebra · Take Apart Numbers

You can use ◯ to take apart 6.
Circle the part you take away.
Then cross it out.

$6 - 5 = \underline{1}$

$6 - 4 = \underline{2}$

Use ◯ to take apart 6. Circle the part you take away. Then cross it out. **Complete the subtraction sentence.**

1. $6 - 3 = \underline{3}$

2. $6 - 2 = \underline{4}$

3. $6 - 1 = \underline{5}$

4. $6 - 0 = \underline{6}$

www.harcourtschoolsupply.com
© Houghton Mifflin Harcourt Publishing Company

21

Core Standards for Math, Grade 1

Lesson 11
CC.1.OA.1

Name _____

1. Which number sentence comes next in the pattern?

$7 - 0 = 7$
$7 - 1 = 6$
$7 - 2 = 5$
$7 - 3 = 4$

○ $7 - 5 = 2$
◉ $7 - 4 = 3$
○ $7 - 3 = 4$
○ $7 - 2 = 5$

2. Which shows a way to take apart 8?

○ $8 + 1 = 9$
○ $9 - 1 = 8$
○ $10 - 2 = 8$
◉ $8 - 6 = 2$

PROBLEM SOLVING REAL WORLD

Solve.

3. Joe has 9 marbles. He gives them all to his sister. How many marbles does he have now?

$\underline{0}$ marbles

www.harcourtschoolsupply.com
© Houghton Mifflin Harcourt Publishing Company

22

Core Standards for Math, Grade 1

Lesson 12
COMMON CORE STANDARD CC.1.OA.1
Lesson Objective: Solve subtraction problem situations using the strategy act it out.

Name _____

Problem Solving · Use Subtraction Strategies

Lara has 15 crackers. She gives some of them away. She has 8 left. How many crackers does she give away?

Unlock the Problem

What do I need to find?	What information do I need to use?
how many <u>crackers</u> Lara gives away	Lara has <u>15</u> crackers. Lara has <u>8</u> crackers left.

Show how to solve the problem.

Lara gives away <u>7</u> crackers.

Act it out to solve. Draw to show your work.

1. Min has 13 marbles. Possible answer:
   She gives some away.
   She has 5 left.
   How many marbles does she give away?

Min gives away <u>8</u> marbles.

www.harcourtschoolsupply.com
© Houghton Mifflin Harcourt Publishing Company

23

Core Standards for Math, Grade 1

Lesson 12
CC.1.OA.1

Name _____

1. Cleo ate 12 cherries. Ben ate 7 cherries. How many fewer cherries did Ben eat than Cleo?

○ 8
○ 7
○ 6
◉ 5

2. Josh picked 11 lemons. He used 4 lemons to make lemonade. How many lemons does Josh have now?

○ 15
○ 8
◉ 7
○ 6

3. Dawn had some chalk. She gave away 5 pieces. Now she has 9 pieces of chalk. How many pieces of chalk did Dawn start with?

◉ 14
○ 9
○ 6
○ 4

4. Mrs. Grasso picks 16 apples. She uses some apples in a pie. She has 9 left. How many apples did Mrs. Grasso use?

○ 6
◉ 7
○ 8
○ 9

Choose a way to solve. Draw or write to explain.

5. Sue has 15 tomatoes. Her family eats some of them. Now Sue has 9 tomatoes. How many did her family eat?   Check children's work.

<u>6</u> tomatoes

www.harcourtschoolsupply.com
© Houghton Mifflin Harcourt Publishing Company

24

Core Standards for Math, Grade 1

Lesson 13

COMMON CORE STANDARD CC.1.OA.1
Lesson Objective: Solve addition and subtraction problem situations using the strategy *make a model*.

Problem Solving • Add or Subtract

There are 12 skunks in the woods.
Some skunks walk away.
There are 8 skunks still in the woods.
How many skunks walk away?

Unlock the Problem

What do I need to find?	**What information do I need to use?**
how many walk away ~~skunks~~	12 skunks in the woods 8 skunks still in the woods

Show how to solve the problem.	
[8] 12	8 skunks still in the woods 12 skunks
4 walk away	

Make a model to solve.
Use 🁢🁢 to help you.

Check children's work.

1. There are 15 frogs on a log.
   Some frogs hop away.
   There are 7 frogs still on the log.
   How many frogs hop away?

7	8
15	

   8 frogs hop away

Lesson 13
CC.1.OA.1

1. Mitchell finds 6 shells on the beach. Now he has 13 shells. How many shells did Mitchell start with?

?	6
13	

   ○ 1   ○ 12
   ● 7   ○ 13

2. Elsa makes 18 cards. She gives some to her friends. Now she has 9 cards left. How many cards does Elsa give to her friends?

   ○ 27   ○ 10
   ○ 11   ● 9

3. Mr. Stuart buys 11 erasers. He gives 7 of them away. How many erasers does he have left?

7	?
11	

   ○ 3   ○ 7
   ● 4   ○ 18

4. Flora has 8 pencils in her pencil case. Pat has 4 more pencils than Flora. How many pencils does Pat have?

   ○ 2   ○ 11
   ○ 4   ● 12

5. Mr. Diaz gives music lessons to 12 children. 5 children are girls. How many children are boys?

   7 boys

Lesson 14

COMMON CORE STANDARD CC.1.OA.1
Lesson Objective: Choose an operation and strategy to solve an addition or subtraction word problem.

Choose an Operation

Liz has 15 stuffed animals. She gives away 6. How many stuffed animals are left?	**THINK** Liz gives some away. So, I subtract. Circle **subtract**.
9 stuffed animals	add (subtract) 15 ⊖ 6 = 9

Circle add or subtract.
Write a number sentence to solve.

1. Misha has 11 crackers.
   He eats 2 crackers.
   How many crackers are left?   add   (subtract)

   9 crackers   11 ⊖ 2 = 9

2. Lynn has 5 shells.
   Dan has 7 shells.
   How many shells do   (add)   subtract
   Lynn and Dan have?

   12 shells   5 ⊕ 7 = 12

Lesson 14
CC.1.OA.1

1. Lisa bakes 6 muffins. Max bakes some more. They bake 14 muffins. Which number sentence shows how many muffins Max bakes?

   ○ 14 + 6 = 20
   ○ 7 + 7 = 14
   ● 14 − 6 = 8
   ○ 14 − 7 = 7

2. Pat sees 6 dogs. Megan sees 4 more dogs than Pat. Which number sentence shows how many dogs they see?

   ○ 6 − 4 = 2
   ○ 6 + 4 + 4 = 14
   ● 6 + 6 + 4 = 16
   ○ 6 + 6 = 12

3. Julia has a fish tank with 12 fish. 4 are clown fish. The rest are goldfish. Which number sentence shows how many goldfish are in the fish tank?

   ● 12 − 4 = 8
   ○ 10 + 2 = 12
   ○ 4 + 2 = 6
   ○ 16 − 12 = 4

4. Jason and Lucy eat 13 raisins. Jason eats 8 raisins. Which number sentence shows how many raisins Lucy eats?

   ○ 13 + 8 = 21
   ○ 9 + 4 = 13
   ○ 5 + 5 = 10
   ● 13 − 8 = 5

5. Jane makes 16 cupcakes. Some have chocolate frosting. 7 have strawberry frosting. How many cupcakes have chocolate frosting?

   16 − 7 = 9, 9 cupcakes

Answer Key

www.harcourtschoolsupply.com
© Houghton Mifflin Harcourt Publishing Company

Name _____

Lesson 15
COMMON CORE STANDARD CC.1.OA.
Lesson Objective: Solve adding to and putting together situations using the strategy *draw a picture.*

Problem Solving •
Use Addition Strategies

Tory has 9 toys. Bob has 4 toys. Joy has 2 toys. How many toys do they have?

Possible drawings are shown.

Unlock the Problem

What do I need to find?	**What information do I need to use?**
how many **toys** they have	Tory has **9** toys. Bob has **4** toys. Joy has **2** toys.

Show how to solve the problem.

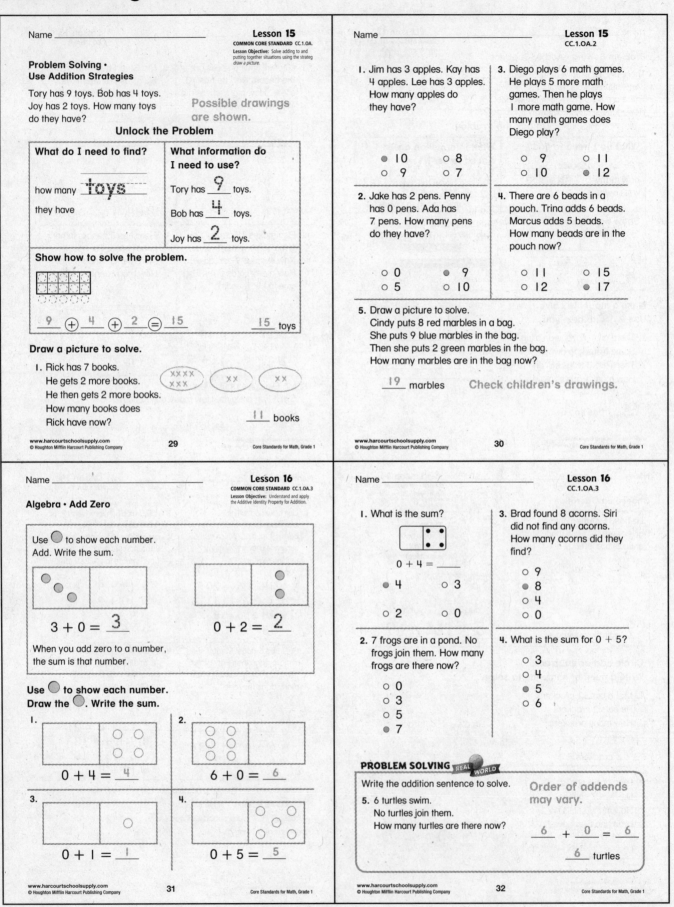

_9_ $(+)$ _4_ $(+)$ _2_ $(=)$ _15_   _15_ toys

Draw a picture to solve.

1. Rick has 7 books.
   He gets 2 more books.
   He then gets 2 more books.
   How many books does
   Rick have now?

   _11_ books

Name _____

Lesson 15
CC.1.OA.2

1. Jim has 3 apples. Kay has 4 apples. Lee has 3 apples. How many apples do they have?

   ● 10   ○ 8
   ○ 9   ○ 7

2. Jake has 2 pens. Penny has 0 pens. Ada has 7 pens. How many pens do they have?

   ○ 0   ● 9
   ○ 5   ○ 10

3. Diego plays 6 math games. He plays 5 more math games. Then he plays 1 more math game. How many math games does Diego play?

   ○ 9   ○ 11
   ○ 10   ● 12

4. There are 6 beads in a pouch. Trina adds 6 beads. Marcus adds 5 beads. How many beads are in the pouch now?

   ○ 11   ○ 15
   ○ 12   ● 17

5. Draw a picture to solve.
   Cindy puts 8 red marbles in a bag.
   She puts 9 blue marbles in the bag.
   Then she puts 2 green marbles in the bag.
   How many marbles are in the bag now?

   _19_ marbles   *Check children's drawings.*

Name _____

Lesson 16
COMMON CORE STANDARD CC.1.OA.3
Lesson Objective: Understand and apply the Additive Identity Property for Addition.

Algebra • Add Zero

Use ⬤ to show each number.
Add. Write the sum.

$3 + 0 = $ _3_ $0 + 2 = $ _2_

When you add zero to a number, the sum is that number.

Use ⬤ to show each number.
Draw the ⬤. Write the sum.

1. $0 + 4 = $ _4_

2. $6 + 0 = $ _6_

3. $0 + 1 = $ _1_

4. $0 + 5 = $ _5_

Name _____

Lesson 16
CC.1.OA.3

1. What is the sum?

   $0 + 4 = $ _____

   ● 4   ○ 3
   ○ 2   ○ 0

2. 7 frogs are in a pond. No frogs join them. How many frogs are there now?

   ○ 0
   ○ 3
   ○ 5
   ● 7

3. Brad found 8 acorns. Siri did not find any acorns. How many acorns did they find?

   ○ 9
   ● 8
   ○ 4
   ○ 0

4. What is the sum for $0 + 5$?

   ○ 3
   ○ 4
   ● 5
   ○ 6

PROBLEM SOLVING REAL WORLD

Write the addition sentence to solve.   *Order of addends may vary.*

5. 6 turtles swim.
   No turtles join them.
   How many turtles are there now?

   _6_ $+$ _0_ $=$ _6_

   _6_ turtles

Lesson 17 (page 33)

Name _____

Lesson 17
COMMON CORE STANDARD CC.1.OA.3
Lesson Objective: Explore the Commutative Property of Addition.

Algebra • Add in Any Order

Write an addition sentence.
Change the order of the addends.
The sum is still the same.

Turn the cube train around.

$5 + 3 = \underset{\text{sum}}{8}$

$\underline{3} + \underline{5} = \underset{\text{sum}}{8}$

Use [cube][cube] to add. Write the sum.

Change the order of the addends. Color to match.
Write the addition sentence.
Check children's coloring.

1.

$1 + 5 = \underline{6}$

$\underline{5} + \underline{1} = \underline{6}$

2.

$3 + 1 = \underline{4}$

$\underline{1} + \underline{3} = \underline{4}$

Lesson 17 (page 34)

Name _____

Lesson 17
CC.1.OA.3

1. Which shows the same addends in a different order?

$3 + 5 = 8$

- ○ $3 + 4 = 7$
- ○ $3 + 5 = 8$
- ○ $5 + 4 = 9$
- ● $5 + 3 = 8$

2. Which shows the same addends in a different order?

$6 + 4 = \underline{}$

- ○ $6 + 6 = \underline{}$
- ○ $6 + 4 = \underline{}$
- ● $4 + 6 = \underline{}$
- ○ $4 + 5 = \underline{}$

3. Which shows the same addends in a different order?

$8 + 2 = 10$

- ○ $2 + 6 = 8$
- ● $2 + 8 = 10$
- ○ $8 + 1 = 9$
- ○ $8 + 2 = 10$

4. Look at the connecting cubes. Which addition fact **cannot** be shown with them?

- ● $5 + 2 = 7$
- ○ $2 + 3 = 5$
- ○ $3 + 2 = 5$
- ○ $0 + 5 = 5$

PROBLEM SOLVING REAL WORLD

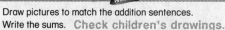

Draw pictures to match the addition sentences.
Write the sums. *Check children's drawings.*

5. $5 + 2 = \underline{7}$

$2 + 5 = \underline{7}$

Lesson 18 (page 35)

Name _____

Lesson 18
COMMON CORE STANDARD CC.1.OA.3
Lesson Objective: Understand and apply the Commutative Property of Addition for sums within 20.

Algebra • Add in Any Order

You can change the order of the addends. The sum is the same.

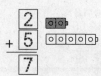

$\begin{array}{r} 5 \\ + 2 \\ \hline 7 \end{array}$

$\begin{array}{r} 2 \\ + 5 \\ \hline 7 \end{array}$

Add. Change the order of the addends. Add again.

1.
$\begin{array}{r} 3 \\ + 1 \\ \hline 4 \end{array}$
$\begin{array}{r} 1 \\ + 3 \\ \hline 4 \end{array}$

2.
$\begin{array}{r} 4 \\ + 2 \\ \hline 6 \end{array}$
$\begin{array}{r} 2 \\ + 4 \\ \hline 6 \end{array}$

3.
$\begin{array}{r} 8 \\ + 3 \\ \hline 11 \end{array}$
$\begin{array}{r} 3 \\ + 8 \\ \hline 11 \end{array}$

4.
$\begin{array}{r} 9 \\ + 5 \\ \hline 14 \end{array}$
$\begin{array}{r} 5 \\ + 9 \\ \hline 14 \end{array}$

Lesson 18 (page 36)

Name _____

Lesson 18
CC.1.OA.3

1. Which shows the same addends in a different order?

$8 + 3 = 11$

- ○ $8 + 2 = 10$
- ● $3 + 8 = 11$
- ○ $7 + 4 = 11$
- ○ $3 + 9 = 12$

2. Which shows the same addends in a different order?

$9 + 4 = 13$

- ● $4 + 9 = 13$
- ○ $5 + 8 = 13$
- ○ $4 + 8 = 12$
- ○ $8 + 3 = 11$

3. Which shows the same addends in a different order?

$7 + 8 = 15$

- ○ $8 + 5 = 13$
- ○ $7 + 7 = 14$
- ○ $9 + 6 = 15$
- ● $8 + 7 = 15$

4. Which shows the same addends in a different order?

$6 + 2 = 8$

- ○ $6 + 4 = 10$
- ○ $3 + 6 = 9$
- ● $2 + 6 = 8$
- ○ $5 + 2 = 7$

5. Add. Change the order of the addends. Add again.

$9 + 6 = \boxed{15}$

$\begin{array}{r} 6 \\ + 9 \\ \hline 15 \end{array}$

Answer Key

Name _____

Lesson 19
COMMON CORE STANDARD CC.1.OA.3
Lesson Objective: Use the Associative Property of Addition to add three addends

Algebra • Add 3 Numbers

You can add numbers in any order.

$3 + 4 + 1 = 8$

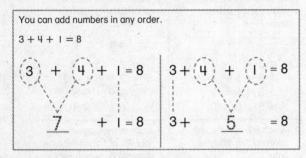

Use circles to change which two addends you add first. Complete the addition sentences.

1. $(2) + (1) + 8 = 11$ $2 + (1) + (8) = 11$

    $\underline{3} + 8 = 11$ $2 + \underline{9} = 11$

2. $(7) + (2) + 3 = 12$ $7 + (2) + (3) = 12$

    $\underline{9} + 3 = 12$ $7 + \underline{5} = 12$

Name _____

Lesson 19
CC.1.OA.3

1. What is the sum of $4 + 1 + 5$?
   - ○ 5
   - ○ 6
   - ○ 9
   - ● 10

2. What is the sum of $2 + 8 + 2$?
   - ○ 6
   - ○ 8
   - ○ 10
   - ● 12

3. What is the sum of $5 + 0 + 3$?
   - ● 8
   - ○ 10
   - ○ 12
   - ○ 14

4. What is the sum of $7 + 3 + 4$?
   - ○ 12
   - ○ 13
   - ● 14
   - ○ 15

PROBLEM SOLVING REAL WORLD

5. Choose three numbers from 1 to 6.
   Write the numbers in an addition sentence.
   Show two ways to find the sum.
   Answers may vary. One possible answer: 3, 4, 6; 3 + 4 + 6 = 13; 7 + 6 = 13; 3 + 10 = 13.

Name _____

Lesson 20
COMMON CORE STANDARD CC.1.OA.3
Lesson Objective: Understand and apply the Associative Property or Commutative Property of Addition to add three addends.

Algebra • Add 3 Numbers

What strategies help you add 3 numbers?

$4 + 6$ make a 10. $4 + 4 = 8$ is a doubles fact.

$\boxed{10} + 4 = \boxed{14}$ $\boxed{8} + 6 = \boxed{14}$

Choose a strategy. Circle two addends to add first. Write the sum. Then find the total sum.

Check children's work.

1. $\begin{array}{r} 7 \\ 3 \\ + 3 \\ \hline 13 \end{array}$ $\boxed{10}$

2. $\begin{array}{r} 2 \\ 2 \\ + 8 \\ \hline \end{array}$ $\boxed{}$ 12

3. $\begin{array}{r} 4 \\ 3 \\ + 3 \\ \hline \end{array}$ $\boxed{}$ 10

4. $\begin{array}{r} 5 \\ 5 \\ + 4 \\ \hline \end{array}$ $\boxed{}$ 14

Name _____

Lesson 20
CC.1.OA.3

1. What is the sum?
   $2 + 6 + 3 = \boxed{}$
   - ○ 13
   - ● 11
   - ○ 9
   - ○ 5

2. What is the sum?
   $6 + 5 + 4 = \boxed{}$
   - ● 15
   - ○ 11
   - ○ 10
   - ○ 9

3. What is the sum?
   $4 + 8 + 4 = \boxed{}$
   - ○ 10
   - ○ 12
   - ○ 14
   - ● 16

4. What is the sum?
   $7 + 1 + 2 = \boxed{}$
   - ○ 8
   - ○ 9
   - ● 10
   - ○ 12

PROBLEM SOLVING REAL WORLD

Draw a picture. Write the number sentence.

5. Don has 4 black dogs.
   Tim has 3 small dogs.
   Sue has 3 big dogs.
   How many dogs do they have?

   Possible drawings shown. Order of addends may vary.

   $\underline{4} + \underline{3} + \underline{3} = \underline{10}$ dogs

---

Answer Key

Name _____ **Lesson 21**

COMMON CORE STANDARD CC.1.OA.4
Lesson Objective: Recall addition facts to subtract numbers within 20.

Think Addition to Subtract

What is 7 − 4?

Think 4 + __3__ = 7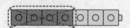

So 7 − 4 = __3__

Use 🟦🟦 **to model the number sentences.**
Draw 🟦🟦 **to show your work.** *Drawings may vary.*

1. What is 11 − 2?

   Think 2 + __9__ = 11

   So 11 − 2 = __9__

2. What is 10 − 6?

   Think 6 + __4__ = 10

   So 10 − 6 = __4__

3. What is 6 − 1?

   Think 1 + __5__ = 6

   So 6 − 1 = __5__

www.harcourtschoolsupply.com
© Houghton Mifflin Harcourt Publishing Company   41   Core Standards for Math, Grade 1

Name _____ **Lesson 21**

CC.1.OA.4

1. Which addition sentence can you use to help you subtract 14 − 8?

   ○ 4 + 4 = 8
   ● 8 + 6 = 14
   ○ 8 + 8 = 16
   ○ 14 + 8 = 22

2. Which addition fact helps solve the subtraction fact 12 − 5?

   ● 7 + 5 = 12
   ○ 12 + 5 = 17
   ○ 5 + 8 = 13
   ○ 6 + 5 = 11

3. Which subtraction sentence can you solve by using 7 + 9 = 16?

   ○ 9 − 7 = 2
   ○ 10 − 6 = 4
   ● 16 − 9 = 7
   ○ 16 − 8 = 8

4. Which addition fact helps solve the subtraction fact 13 − 4?

   ○ 8 + 6 = 14
   ○ 8 + 5 = 13
   ○ 9 + 3 = 12
   ● 9 + 4 = 13

PROBLEM SOLVING REAL WORLD

5. Write a number sentence to solve.
   I have 18 pieces of fruit.
   9 are apples.
   The rest are oranges.
   How many are oranges?

   Also accept 9 + 9 = 18.

   18 ⊖ 9 ⊜ 9

   __9__ oranges

www.harcourtschoolsupply.com
© Houghton Mifflin Harcourt Publishing Company   42   Core Standards for Math, Grade 1

Name _____ **Lesson 22**

COMMON CORE STANDARD CC.1.OA.4
Lesson Objective: Use addition as a strategy to subtract numbers within 20.

Use Think Addition to Subtract

Think of an addition fact to help you subtract.	Think

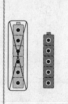

11 − 6 = __?__ | 6 + __5__ = 11 | 11 − 6 = __5__

Use an addition fact to help you subtract.

1. What is 9 − 4?

   Use 4 + __5__ = 9

   So 9 − 4 = __5__

2. What is 10 − 6?

   Use 6 + __4__ = 10

   So 10 − 6 = __4__

3. What is 12 − 5?

   Use 5 + __7__ = 12

   So 12 − 5 = __7__

4. What is 8 − 5?

   Use 5 + __3__ = 8

   So 8 − 5 = __3__

www.harcourtschoolsupply.com
© Houghton Mifflin Harcourt Publishing Company   43   Core Standards for Math, Grade 1

Name _____ **Lesson 22**

CC.1.OA.4

1. Which addition fact can you use to help you subtract 11 − 6?

   ○ 6 + 1 = 7
   ○ 10 + 1 = 11
   ● 5 + 6 = 11
   ○ 11 + 6 = 17

2. What number is missing?

   6   14
   + 8   − 8
   ____   ____
   14   □

   ● 6
   ○ 8
   ○ 10
   ○ 14

3. Maria has 18 pears. She gives some of them away. She has 9 pears left. How many pears does Maria give away?

   ○ 27
   ○ 18
   ○ 10
   ● 9

4. Which subtraction sentence can you solve by using 9 + 6 = 15?

   ● 15 − 6 = ____
   ○ 15 − 7 = ____
   ○ 9 − 6 = ____
   ○ 16 − 9 = ____

PROBLEM SOLVING REAL WORLD

5. Solve. Draw or write to show your work.
   I have 15 nickels.
   Some are old. 6 are new.
   How many nickels are old?

   Check children's work.

   __9__ nickels

www.harcourtschoolsupply.com
© Houghton Mifflin Harcourt Publishing Company   44   Core Standards for Math, Grade 1

---

www.harcourtschoolsupply.com

© Houghton Mifflin Harcourt Publishing Company

211

Core Standards for Math, Grade 1

Answer Key

Name _____

Lesson 23
COMMON CORE STANDARD CC.1.OA.5
Lesson Objective: Use count on 1, 2, or 3 as a strategy to find sums within 20.

Count On

You can count on to find $4 + 3$.
Start with the greater addend.
Then count on. Write the sum.

To add 3, count on 3.

⬜**4**   ○5 ○6 ○7

$4 + 3 = 7$

Circle the greater addend. Count on 1, 2, or 3.
Write the missing numbers.

1. $1 + 6$
○ ○
⬜6 7
$1 + ⑥ = 7$

2. $9 + 1$
○ ○
⬜9 10
$⑨ + 1 = 10$

3. $4 + 2$
○ ○ ○
⬜4 5 6
$④ + 2 = 6$

4. $3 + 8$
○ ○ ○
⬜8 9 10 11
$3 + ⑧ = 11$

Name _____

Lesson 23
CC.1.OA.5

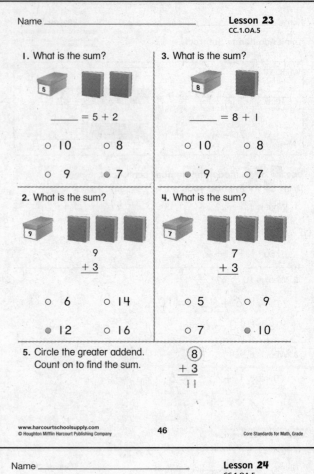

1. What is the sum?
_____ $= 5 + 2$
○ 10   ○ 8
○ 9   ● 7

3. What is the sum?
_____ $= 8 + 1$
○ 10   ○ 8
● 9   ○ 7

2. What is the sum?
9
$+3$
○ 6   ○ 14
● 12   ○ 16

4. What is the sum?
7
$+3$
○ 5   ○ 9
○ 7   ● 10

5. Circle the greater addend.
Count on to find the sum.
⑧
$+3$
11

Name _____

Lesson 24
COMMON CORE STANDARD CC.1.OA.5
Lesson Objective: Use count back 1, 2, or 3 as a strategy to subtract.

Count Back

Count back to subtract.

Use 9 ●. Count back 3.
This shows counting back 3 from 9.

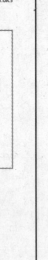

6 7 8 9

$9 - 3 = 6$

Use ●. Count back 1, 2, or 3.
Write the difference.

1. $5 - 1 = 4$
4 5

2. $7 - 2 = 5$
5 6 7

3. $6 - 3 = 3$
3 4 5 6

Name _____

Lesson 24
CC.1.OA.5

1. Count back. What is the difference?
$10 - 2 = ⬜$
● 8
○ 9
○ 10
○ 12

3. Luis had 11 markers. He gave 2 markers to Elena. How many markers does Luis have now?
○ 13
○ 10
● 9
○ 8

2. Count back. What is the difference?
$9 - 3 = ⬜$
○ 5
● 6
○ 7
○ 8

4. Vicky made 8 muffins. Her family ate some. Now there are 5 muffins. How many muffins did her family eat? Which subtraction sentence answers the problem?
○ $5 - 3 = 2$
○ $10 - 5 = 5$
● $8 - 3 = 5$
○ $8 - 2 = 6$

PROBLEM SOLVING

Write a subtraction sentence to solve.

5. Tina has 12 pencils. She gives away 3 pencils. How many pencils are left?
$12 - 3 = 9$
9 pencils

Lesson 25
COMMON CORE STANDARD CC.1.OA.6
Lesson Objective: Build fluency for addition within 10.

Name _____

Addition to 10

You can use ▢ to help you add.

```
  4  [oooo]
+ 2  [oo]
  6
```

```
  6  [oooooo]
+ 3  [ooo]
  9
```

Use ▢. Write the sum.

1.
```
  1  [o]
+ 2  [oo]
  3
```

2.
```
  4  [oooo]
+ 1  [o]
  5
```

3.
```
  3  [ooo]
+ 5  [ooooo]
  8
```

4.
```
  2  [oo]
+ 3  [ooo]
  5
```

Name _____

Lesson 25
CC.1.OA.6

1. What is the sum?
```
  3
+ 7
```
- ○ 8
- ○ 9
- ◉ 10
- ○ 11

3. What is the sum?
```
  5
+ 4
```
- ○ 3
- ○ 8
- ◉ 9
- ○ 10

2. What is the sum?
```
  4
+ 4
```
- ○ 4
- ○ 6
- ○ 7
- ◉ 8

4. What is the sum?
```
  0
+ 1
```
- ○ 0
- ○ 1
- ◉ 2
- ○ 10

PROBLEM SOLVING REAL WORLD

Add. Write the sum. Use the sum and the key to color the flowers.

5.

```
  2
+ 5
  7
```
4 + 5 = 9
```
  7
+ 1
  8
```

KEY
- 6 — YELLOW
- 7 — RED
- 8 — PURPLE
- 9 — PINK

Name _____

Lesson 26
COMMON CORE STANDARD CC.1.OA.6
Lesson Objective: Build fluency for subtraction within 10.

Subtraction from 10 or Less

You can use ▢ to help you subtract.

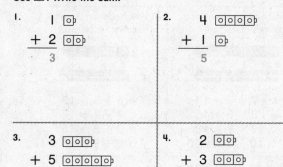

```
  6
- 3
  3
```

```
  3
- 1
  2
```

Write the subtraction problem.

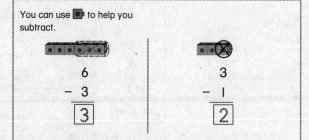

1.
```
  7
- 4
  3
```

2.
```
  5
- 3
  2
```

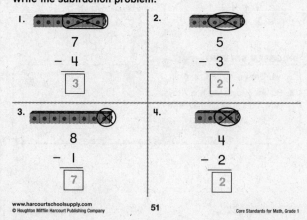

3.
```
  8
- 1
  7
```

4.
```
  4
- 2
  2
```

Name _____

Lesson 26
CC.1.OA.6

1. What is the difference?
```
  6
- 5
```
- ○ 4
- ○ 3
- ○ 2
- ◉ 1

2. What is the difference?
```
 10
- 7
```
- ○ 4
- ◉ 3
- ○ 2
- ○ 0

PROBLEM SOLVING REAL WORLD

Solve.

3. 6 birds are in the tree.
   None of the birds fly away.
   How many birds are left?

   6 − 0 = 6

Answer Key

Add Doubles

The addends are the same in a doubles fact.

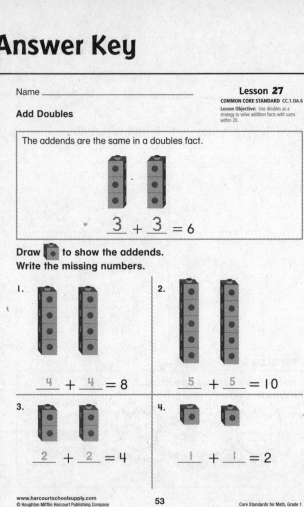

$\underline{3} + \underline{3} = 6$

Draw to show the addends.
Write the missing numbers.

1. $\underline{4} + \underline{4} = 8$

2. $\underline{5} + \underline{5} = 10$

3. $\underline{2} + \underline{2} = 4$

4. $\underline{1} + \underline{1} = 2$

---

1. Which addition sentence matches the picture?
- ○ $3 + 3 = 6$
- ○ $4 + 4 = 8$
- ● $5 + 5 = 10$
- ○ $6 + 6 = 12$

3. Which addition sentence matches the picture?
- ○ $4 + 4 = 8$
- ● $3 + 3 = 6$
- ○ $2 + 2 = 4$
- ○ $1 + 1 = 2$

2. Which addition sentence matches the picture?
- ○ $7 + 7 = 14$
- ● $8 + 8 = 16$
- ○ $9 + 9 = 18$
- ○ $10 + 10 = 20$

4. Which addition sentence matches the picture?
- ● $6 + 6 = 12$
- ○ $7 + 7 = 14$
- ○ $8 + 8 = 16$
- ○ $9 + 9 = 18$

5. Write the doubles fact that matches the picture.

$\underline{7} + \underline{7} = \underline{14}$

Use Doubles to Add

Use a doubles fact to solve $4 + 3$.
Break apart 4 into $1 + 3$.

THINK
$3 + 3 = 6$.
1 more than 6 is 7.

$1 + 3 + 3$
$1 + 6 = 7$

So, $4 + 3 = \underline{7}$.

Use ○● **to model. Break apart to make a doubles fact. Add.**

1. $6 + 5$

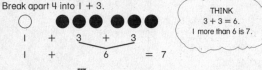

$1 + \underline{5} + \underline{5}$
$1 + \underline{10} = \underline{11}$

So, $6 + 5 = \underline{11}$.

2. $8 + 7$

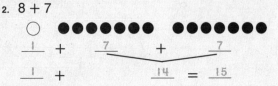

$1 + \underline{7} + \underline{7}$
$1 + \underline{14} = \underline{15}$

So, $8 + 7 = \underline{15}$.

---

1. Which has the same sum as $7 + 6$?
- ○ $1 + 7 + 7$
- ● $1 + 6 + 6$
- ○ $4 + 4 + 2$
- ○ $3 + 3 + 3$

3. Which has the same sum as $7 + 8$?
- ○ $3 + 3 + 1$
- ○ $4 + 4 + 1$
- ● $7 + 7 + 1$
- ○ $8 + 8 + 2$

2. Which has the same sum as $4 + 3$?
- ○ $7 + 7 + 1$
- ○ $5 + 5 + 1$
- ○ $4 + 4 + 1$
- ● $1 + 3 + 3$

4. Which has the same sum as $5 + 6$?
- ○ $5 + 1 + 6$
- ● $5 + 5 + 1$
- ○ $6 + 5 + 5$
- ○ $6 + 6 + 5$

PROBLEM SOLVING REAL WORLD

Solve. Draw or write to explain.

5. Bo has 6 toys. Mia has 7 toys. How many toys do they have?

$\underline{13}$ toys

Answer Key

Lesson 29

Name _____

COMMON CORE STANDARD CC.1.OA.6
Lesson Objective: Use doubles plus 1 and doubles minus 1 as strategies to find sums within 20.

Doubles Plus 1 and Doubles Minus 1

You can use doubles plus one facts and doubles minus one to add.

Use doubles fact 3 + 3 = 6.

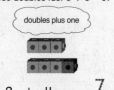

doubles plus one

doubles minus one

$3 + 4 = \underline{7}$ $3 + 2 = \underline{5}$

Use doubles plus one or doubles minus one to add.

1.

$5 + 6 = \underline{11}$ $5 + 4 = \underline{9}$

2.

$2 + 3 = \underline{5}$ $2 + 1 = \underline{3}$

Name _____   **Lesson 29**   CC.1.OA.6

1. Which doubles fact helps you solve 3 + 4 = 7?
   - ● 4 + 4 = 8
   - ○ 5 + 5 = 10
   - ○ 6 + 6 = 12
   - ○ 7 + 7 = 14

2. Which doubles fact helps you solve 5 + 4 = 9?
   - ○ 3 + 3 = 6
   - ● 4 + 4 = 8
   - ○ 6 + 6 = 12
   - ○ 7 + 7 = 14

3. Which doubles fact helps you solve 7 + 6 = 13?
   - ○ 5 + 5 = 10
   - ● 6 + 6 = 12
   - ○ 8 + 8 = 16
   - ○ 9 + 9 = 18

4. Which doubles fact helps you solve 8 + 9 = 17?
   - ○ 5 + 5 = 10
   - ○ 6 + 6 = 12
   - ○ 7 + 7 = 14
   - ● 9 + 9 = 18

PROBLEM SOLVING REAL WORLD

5. Andy writes an addition fact. One addend is 9. The sum is 17. What is the other addend? Write the addition fact.

$\underline{9} + \underline{8} = 17$ or 8 + 9 = 17

Name _____   **Lesson 30**

COMMON CORE STANDARD CC.1.OA.6
Lesson Objective: Use the strategies count on, doubles, doubles plus 1, and doubles minus 1 to practice addition facts within 20.

Practice the Strategies

You can use different addition strategies to find sums.

Count On

6 7 8

$6 + 2 = \underline{8}$

Doubles

$3 + 3 = \underline{6}$

Doubles Plus 1

$5 + 6 = \underline{11}$

Doubles Minus 1

$5 + 4 = \underline{9}$

1. Count on 1.
$7 + 1 = \underline{8}$

2. Count on 2.
$7 + 2 = \underline{9}$

3. Count on 3.
$7 + 3 = \underline{10}$

4. Use doubles.
$6 + 6 = \underline{12}$

5. Use doubles plus 1.
$6 + 7 = \underline{13}$

6. Use doubles minus 1.
$6 + 5 = \underline{11}$

Name _____   **Lesson 30**   CC.1.OA.6

1. What is the missing sum?

Doubles
3 + 3 = 6
4 + 4 = 8
5 + 5 = 10
6 + 6 = ____

- ● 12
- ○ 14
- ○ 16
- ○ 18

2. What is the missing sum?

Doubles Plus One
6 + 7 = 13
7 + 8 = 15
8 + 9 = ____

- ○ 15
- ○ 16
- ● 17
- ○ 18

3. What is the missing sum?

Count On 3
3 + 3 = 6
4 + 3 = 7
5 + 3 = 8
6 + 3 = ____

- ○ 6
- ○ 7
- ○ 8
- ● 9

4. What is the missing sum?

Doubles Minus One
3 + 2 = 5
4 + 3 = 7
5 + 4 = ____

- ○ 8
- ● 9
- ○ 10
- ○ 11

5. What is the sum?

$8 + 3 = \underline{11}$

Answer Key

Lesson 31
COMMON CORE STANDARD CC.1.OA.6
Lesson Objective: Use a ten frame to add 10 and an addend less than 10.

Add 10 and More

You can use counters and a ten frame to add a number to 10.

Find 10 + 4.

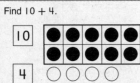

```
  10
+  4
 14
```

Draw ◯. Show the number that is added to 10.
Write the sum.

1.

```
  10
+  3
 13
```

2.

```
  10
+  7
 17
```

Lesson 31
CC.1.OA.6

1. What number sentence does this model show?

- ◦ 10 − 4 = 6
- ◦ 5 + 4 = 9
- ◦ 7 + 6 = 13
- ● 10 + 4 = 14

3. What number sentence does this model show?

- ◦ 5 + 2 = 7
- ◦ 12 − 3 = 9
- ● 10 + 2 = 12
- ◦ 10 + 3 = 13

2. What number sentence does this model show?

- ● 10 + 7 = 17
- ◦ 10 + 5 = 15
- ◦ 5 + 2 = 7
- ◦ 10 − 7 = 3

4. What number sentence does this model show?

- ◦ 5 + 5 = 10
- ◦ 10 − 5 = 5
- ● 10 + 5 = 15
- ◦ 10 + 10 = 20

5. Draw ● to show 10.
Draw ◯ to show the other addend. Write the sum.

```
  10
+  6
 16
```

Lesson 32
COMMON CORE STANDARD CC.1.OA.6
Lesson Objective: Use make a ten as a strategy to find sums within 20.

Make a 10 to Add

Show 8 + 5 with counters and a ten frame.

Use ◯.

Make a ten. Add.

```
  10
+  3
 13
```

So, 8 + 5 = **13**.

Draw ◯ to show the second addend. Make a ten. Add.

1. 8 + 6

```
  10
+  4
 14
```

So, 8 + 6 = **14**.

2. 9 + 7

```
  10
+  6
 16
```

So, 9 + 7 = **16**.

Lesson 32
CC.1.OA.6

1. What number sentence does this model show?

- ◦ 7 − 3 = 4
- ● 7 + 6 = 13
- ◦ 10 + 3 = 13
- ◦ 10 + 7 = 17

3. What number sentence does this model show?

- ◦ 9 − 5 = 4
- ◦ 15 − 5 = 10
- ● 6 + 9 = 15
- ◦ 6 + 10 = 16

2. What number sentence does this model show?

- ◦ 7 + 7 = 14
- ◦ 14 − 4 = 10
- ◦ 8 + 4 = 12
- ● 8 + 6 = 14

4. What number sentence does this model show?

- ● 9 + 8 = 17
- ◦ 9 + 7 = 16
- ◦ 9 + 5 = 14
- ◦ 17 − 7 = 10

PROBLEM SOLVING REAL WORLD

Solve.

5. 10 + 6 has the same sum as 7 + **9**.

Lesson 33

COMMON CORE STANDARD CC.1.OA.6
Lesson Objective: Use numbers to show how to use the make a ten strategy to add.

Name _____

Use Make a 10 to Add

What is 9 + 5? Make a 10 to add.

Use ◯ and a ten frame. Show the addends.

9
5

Show the greater addend in the ten frame.

Make a 10. Add.

10
4

So, 9 + 5 = 14.

Draw ◯. Make a ten to add.

1. 8 + 5

8
5

10
3

10
+ 3
13

So, 8 + 5 = 13.

2. 7 + 4

7
4

10
1

10
+ 1
11

So, 7 + 4 = 11.

Lesson 33
CC.1.OA.6

Name _____

1. Which shows a way to make a ten to solve 9 + 3?

○ 9 + 1 + 3
◉ 9 + 1 + 2
○ 5 + 5 + 3
○ 3 + 7 + 3

3. Which shows a way to make a ten to solve 8 + 4?

○ 5 + 3 + 2
○ 5 + 5 + 4
○ 8 + 1 + 2
◉ 8 + 2 + 2

2. Which shows a way to make a ten to solve 9 + 6?

○ 5 + 4 + 5
○ 6 + 6 + 4
◉ 9 + 1 + 5
○ 5 + 5 + 6

4. Which shows a way to make a ten to solve 6 + 5?

◉ 6 + 4 + 1
○ 6 + 4 + 4
○ 5 + 5 + 5
○ 5 + 4 + 1

5. Write to show how you make a ten. Then add. What is 9 + 7?

9 + 1 + 6
10 + 6 = 16
So, 9 + 7 = 16

Lesson 34

COMMON CORE STANDARD CC.1.OA.6
Lesson Objective: Use make a 10 as a strategy to subtract.

Name _____

Use 10 to Subtract

Find 14 − 9.

Start with 9 cubes.

Make a 10.

Add cubes to make 14.

Count what you added.

You added 5

So, 14 − 9 = 5

Use ⬛. Make a ten to subtract.
Draw to show your work. Check children's drawings.

1. 12 − 8 = ?

12 − 8 = 4

2. 15 − 9 = ?

15 − 9 = 6

Lesson 34
CC.1.OA.6

Name _____

1. Use ten frames to make a ten to help you subtract.

15 − 9 = ?

7 ○   6 ◉   5 ○   4 ○

2. Use ten frames to make a ten to help you subtract. Angel has 16 grapes. He eats some of them. He has 7 grapes left. How many grapes did Angel eat?

9 ◉   8 ○   7 ○   6 ○

3. Mr. Dunn had 12 eggs. He used 8 eggs for breakfast. How many eggs are left?

20 ○   6 ○   4 ◉   2 ○

4. Write the number sentence that matches the subtraction shown in the ten frames.

17 − 8 = 9

Answer Key

Core Standards for Math, Grade 1

Name _____

Lesson 35
COMMON CORE STANDARD CC.1.OA.6
Lesson Objective: Subtract by breaking apart to make a ten.

Break Apart to Subtract

What is 14 − 5?

Start with 14. Make a ten.

Take __4__ from 14.

$\underline{14} - \underline{4} = \underline{10}$

Step 1

Then take __1__ more.

$\underline{10} - \underline{1} = \underline{9}$

Step 2

So, 14 − 5 = __9__

Subtract.

1. What is 17 − 9?

Take 7 counters from 17.

Step 1

17 − 7 = __10__

Then take __2__ counters from 10.

Step 2

$\underline{10} - \underline{2} = \underline{8}$

So, 17 − 9 = __8__

69
Core Standards for Math, Grade 1

Name _____

Lesson 35
CC.1.OA.6

1. Ray uses ten frames to find 15 − 7. Which is the correct answer?

- ○ 5
- ○ 6
- ○ 7
- ● 8

3. Rosa uses ten frames to find 16 − 9. How many will she subtract first from 16 to get to 10?

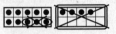

- ● 6
- ○ 7
- ○ 8
- ○ 9

2. Make a ten to solve. What is 13 − 5?

- ○ 3
- ○ 5
- ● 8
- ○ 9

4. Make a ten to solve. What is 14 − 7?

- ○ 4
- ○ 6
- ● 7
- ○ 8

5. There are 13 birds in the tree. 8 birds fly away. How many birds are still in the tree?

$\underline{13} - \underline{8} = \underline{5}$

__5__ birds

70
Core Standards for Math, Grade 1

Name _____

Lesson 36
COMMON CORE STANDARD CC.1.OA.6
Lesson Objective: Record related facts within 20.

Record Related Facts

Use the numbers to write four related facts.

THINK
Each number is in all four facts.

6 + 4 = 10   10 − 4 = 6

4 + 6 = 10   10 − 6 = 4

Use the numbers to make related facts.

1.
6 + 8 = 14   14 − 8 = 6
8 + 6 = 14   14 − 6 = 8

2.
2 + 7 = 9   9 − 7 = 2
7 + 2 = 9   9 − 2 = 7

3.
5 + 6 = 11   11 − 6 = 5
6 + 5 = 11   11 − 5 = 6

4.
3 + 9 = 12   12 − 9 = 3
9 + 3 = 12   12 − 3 = 9

71
Core Standards for Math, Grade 1

Name _____

Lesson 36
CC.1.OA.6

1. What is the missing number?

☐ + 3 = 11

11 − 3 = ☐

3 + ☐ = 11

11 − ☐ = 3

- ○ 3
- ● 8
- ○ 9
- ○ 15

3. Which fact is a related fact?

8 + 7 = 15

15 − 7 = 8

- ● 15 − 8 = 7
- ○ 8 − 6 = 2
- ○ 7 + 7 = 14
- ○ 8 + 4 = 12

2. What is the missing number?

☐ + 4 = 12

12 − 4 = ☐

4 + ☐ = 12

12 − ☐ = 4

- ○ 6
- ● 8
- ○ 10
- ○ 13

4. Which fact is a related fact?

5 + 6 = 11

11 − 6 = 5

- ○ 5 + 8 = 13
- ○ 6 − 5 = 1
- ○ 6 + 6 = 12
- ● 11 − 5 = 6

5. Write the missing related fact.

9 + 6 = 15   15 − 9 = 6

6 + 9 = 15   15 − 6 = 9

72
Core Standards for Math, Grade 1

Lesson 37
COMMON CORE STANDARD CC.1.OA.6
Lesson Objective: Identify related addition and subtraction facts within 20.

Name _____

Identify Related Facts

If you know an addition fact, you will also know the related subtraction fact.

Both facts use 2, 4, and 6. They are related facts.

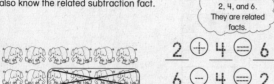

$2 \oplus 4 \ominus 6$

$6 \ominus 4 \ominus 2$

Add and subtract the related facts.

1.

$7 + 8 = \underline{15}$

$15 - 8 = \underline{7}$

2.

$7 + 4 = \underline{11}$

$11 - 4 = \underline{7}$

3.

$1 + 8 = \underline{9}$

$9 - 8 = \underline{1}$

Lesson 37
CC.1.OA.6

Name _____

1. Look at the pairs of facts. Which shows related facts?

$6 + 5 = 11 \qquad 6 - 1 = 5$
$5 + 1 = 6 \qquad 5 + 1 = 6$
○   ●

$6 + 5 = 11 \qquad 16 - 8 = 8$
$5 + 5 = 10 \qquad 5 + 9 = 14$
○   ○

2. Look at the pairs of facts. Which shows related facts?

$7 + 7 = 14 \qquad 7 + 8 = 15$
$8 + 8 = 16 \qquad 8 + 9 = 17$
○   ○

$7 + 7 = 14 \qquad 1 + 7 = 8$
$14 - 7 = 7 \qquad 17 - 8 = 9$
●   ○

3. Which subtraction fact is related to $8 + 5 = 13$?

○ $8 - 5 = 3$
○ $13 - 4 = 9$
○ $13 - 6 = 7$
● $13 - 5 = 8$

4. Which addition fact is related to $10 - 7 = 3$?

● $3 + 7 = 10$
○ $3 + 5 = 8$
○ $7 + 7 = 14$
○ $10 + 3 = 13$

5. Look at the addition fact.

$8 + 8 = 16$

Write a related subtraction fact.

$\underline{16 - 8 = 8}$

Lesson 38
COMMON CORE STANDARD CC.1.OA.6
Lesson Objective: Apply the inverse relationship of addition and subtraction.

Name _____

Use Addition to Check Subtraction

You can use addition to check subtraction.

You start with 8.
Take apart to subtract.

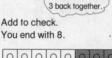

$\begin{array}{r} 8 \\ - 3 \\ \hline \boxed{5} \end{array}$

THINK Put the 5 and 3 back together.

Add to check.
You end with 8.

$\begin{array}{r} \boxed{5} \\ + 3 \\ \hline \boxed{8} \end{array}$

Use 🔲🔳 to help you. Subtract.
Then add to check your answer.

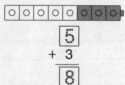

$\begin{array}{r} 7 \\ - 3 \\ \hline \boxed{4} \end{array}$

$\begin{array}{r} \boxed{4} \\ + 3 \\ \hline \boxed{7} \end{array}$

Lesson 38
CC.1.OA.6

Name _____

1. Which addition fact can you use to check the subtraction?

$14 - 6 = \boxed{}$

● $8 + 6 = 14$
○ $8 + 3 = 11$
○ $3 + 9 = 12$
○ $7 + 7 = 14$

2. Which addition fact can you use to check the subtraction?

$16 - 8 = \boxed{}$

○ $4 + 8 = 12$
○ $3 + 8 = 11$
○ $6 + 9 = 15$
● $8 + 8 = 16$

3. Which addition fact can you use to check the subtraction?

$10 - 4 = 6$

○ $8 + 8 = 16$
● $6 + 4 = 10$
○ $9 + 4 = 13$
○ $6 + 6 = 12$

4. Which addition fact can you use to check the subtraction?

$12 - 9 = 3$

○ $3 + 3 = 6$
● $3 + 9 = 12$
○ $9 + 9 = 18$
○ $3 + 6 = 9$

5. Subtract. Then add to check your answer.

$13 - 8 = \boxed{5}$

$\underline{5} + \underline{8} = \boxed{13}$

or $8 + 5 = 13$

Answer Key

Name _____

Lesson 39
COMMON CORE STANDARD CC.1.OA.6
Lesson Objective: Represent equivalent forms of numbers using sums and differences within 20.

Algebra • Ways to Make Numbers to 20

These are some ways to make the number 14.

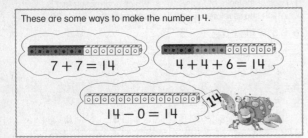

$7 + 7 = 14$ $4 + 4 + 6 = 14$

$14 - 0 = 14$

Use ⬚ ⬚⬚ to show each way.
Cross out the way that does not make the number.

1. 7	$8 - 1$	$3 + 4$	$2 + 3 + 1$
2. 15	~~$7 + 6$~~	$15 - 0$	$8 + 7$
3. 13	$4 + 4 + 5$	~~$9 - 4$~~	$6 + 7$
4. 9	~~$8 + 2$~~	$3 + 3 + 3$	$10 - 1$
5. 18	$9 + 9$	~~$9 - 9$~~	$18 - 0$

Name _____

Lesson 39
CC.1.OA.6

1. The table shows ways to make 14. Which shows a different way to make 14?

14
$7 + 7$
$3 + 6 + 5$

● $8 + 6$ ○ $15 - 0$
○ $9 + 6$ ○ $12 - 7$

2. The table shows ways to make 18. Which shows a different way to make 18?

18
$9 + 9$
$4 + 6 + 8$

○ $10 + 5$ ○ $19 - 3$
○ $15 + 1$ ● $10 + 8$

3. Which way makes 13?

● $7 + 6$
○ $15 - 6$
○ $11 - 2$
○ $7 + 7$

4. Which way makes 15?

○ $6 + 7 + 3$
○ $10 - 5$
○ $8 + 5$
● $7 + 3 + 5$

5. Write two ways to make 12.   Possible answers given.

$6 + 6 = 12$ $3 + 7 + 2 = 12$

Name _____

Lesson 40
COMMON CORE STANDARD CC.1.OA.6
Lesson Objective: Add and subtract facts within 20 and demonstrate fluency for addition and subtraction within 10.

Basic Facts to 20

Mr. Chi has 12 books.
He sells 3 books.
How many books are left?
What is $12 - 3$?

THINK
I can count back.

Start at 12.
Count 11, 10, _9_.

THINK
I can use a related fact.

$3 + 9 = 12$
$12 - 3 = \underline{9}$

So, $12 - 3 = \underline{9}$.

Add or subtract.

1. $14 - 5 = \underline{9}$ 2. $9 + 2 = \underline{11}$ 3. $6 + 4 = \underline{10}$

4. $12 - 6 = \underline{3}$ 5. $8 - 3 = \underline{5}$ 6. $7 + 5 = \underline{12}$

7. $9 + 6 = \underline{15}$ 8. $13 - 9 = \underline{4}$ 9. $8 + 8 = \underline{16}$

Name _____

Lesson 40
CC.1.OA.6

1. There are 13 frogs in a pond. Then 8 frogs hop away. How many frogs are still in the pond?

● 5
○ 6
○ 7
○ 8

2. There are 8 cows at the farm. Then 4 cows come. How many cows are there now?

○ 9
○ 10
○ 11
● 12

3. What is $14 - 5$?

○ 7
○ 8
● 9
○ 10

4. What is $8 + 6$?

○ 12
○ 13
● 14
○ 15

PROBLEM SOLVING REAL WORLD

Solve. Draw or write to explain.

5. Kara has 9 drawings. She gives 4 away. How many drawings does Kara have now?

_5_ drawings

Answer Key

Name _____

Lesson 41
COMMON CORE STANDARD CC.1.OA.6
Lesson Objective: Add and subtract within 20

Add and Subtract within 20

You can use strategies to add or subtract.
- count on
- doubles
- doubles plus one
- count back
- related facts
- doubles minus one

What is $5 + 6$?

I can use doubles plus one.

$5 + 5 = 10$

$$So, 5 + 6 = \underline{11}.$$

What is $12 - 4$?

I can use a related fact.

$8 + 4 = 12$

$$So, 12 - 4 = \underline{8}.$$

Add or subtract.

1. $12 - 3 = \underline{9}$
2. $8 + 9 = \underline{17}$
3. $10 - 5 = \underline{5}$
4. $13 - 7 = \underline{6}$
5. $7 + 8 = \underline{15}$
6. $6 + 6 = \underline{12}$

Name _____

Lesson 41
CC.1.OA.6

1. Add.

$4 + 5 = \underline{}$

- ○ 8
- ● 9
- ○ 10
- ○ 11

2. Subtract.

$10 - 6 = \underline{}$

- ○ 6
- ○ 5
- ● 4
- ○ 3

3. What is the missing number?

$9 + \underline{} = 18$

- ○ 7
- ○ 8
- ● 9
- ○ 10

4. What is the missing number?

$12 - \underline{} = 7$

- ○ 9
- ○ 7
- ○ 6
- ● 5

PROBLEM SOLVING REAL WORLD

Solve. Draw or write to explain.

5. Jesse has 4 shells. He finds some more. Now he has 12 shells. How many more shells did Jesse find?

Check children's work.

$12 - 4 = 8$

$\underline{8}$ more shells

Name _____

Lesson 42
COMMON CORE STANDARD CC.1.OA.7
Lesson Objective: Determine if an equation is true or false.

Algebra • Equal and Not Equal

An equal sign means both sides are the same.

$3 + 3 = 6 - 0$

THINK
$3 + 3 = 6$ and $6 - 0 = 6$.
Is 6 the same as 6?
yes
It is true.

$3 + 2 = 5 - 2$

THINK
$3 + 2 = 5$ and $5 - 2 = 3$.
Is 5 the same as 3?
no
It is false.

Which is true? Circle your answer.
Which is false? Cross out your answer.

1. ~~$7 - 5 = 5 - 2$~~
   ⟨$8 - 8 = 6 - 6$⟩

2. ~~$1 + 8 = 18$~~
   ⟨$2 + 8 = 8 + 2$⟩

3. ⟨$4 + 3 = 5 + 2$⟩
   ~~$7 + 3 = 4 + 5$~~

4. ~~$9 - 2 = 9 + 2$~~
   ⟨$9 = 10 - 1$⟩

Name _____

Lesson 42
CC.1.OA.7

1. Which makes the sentence true?

$10 - 4 = 2 + \square$

- ○ 3
- ● 4
- ○ 5
- ○ 6

2. Which makes the sentence true?

$12 - 0 = 6 + \square$

- ○ 4
- ○ 5
- ● 6
- ○ 7

3. Which makes the sentence true?

$16 - 7 = 8 + \square$

- ● 1
- ○ 2
- ○ 3
- ○ 4

4. Which makes the sentence true?

$8 + 2 = \underline{}$

- ○ $10 - 1$
- ● $5 + 5$
- ○ $13 - 4$
- ○ $3 + 8$

5. Write two numbers to make the sentence true.

$8 + 6 = \underline{} + \underline{}$

Answers will vary.
Check children's work.

Answer Key

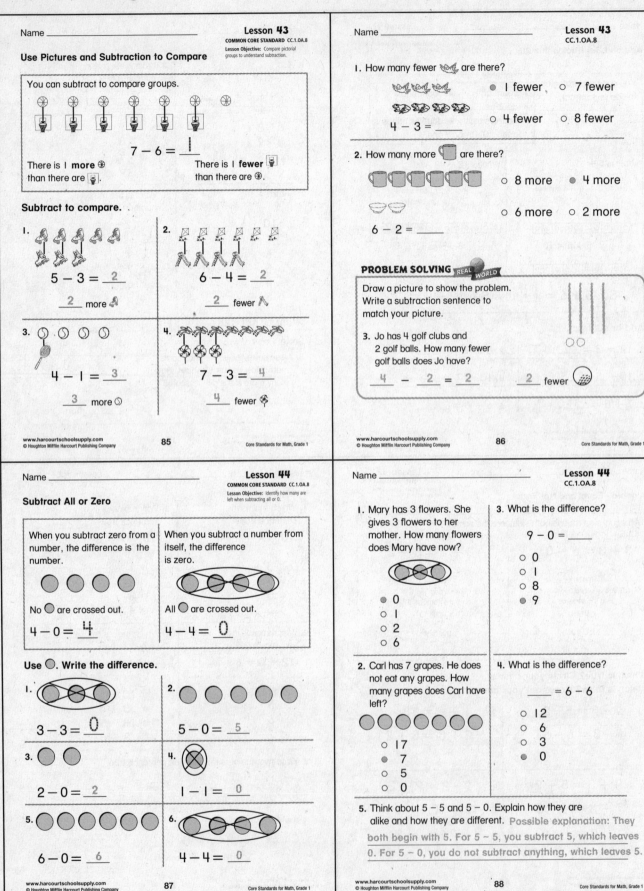

Lesson 43
COMMON CORE STANDARD CC.1.OA.8
Lesson Objective: Compare pictorial groups to understand subtraction.

Use Pictures and Subtraction to Compare

You can subtract to compare groups.

$7 - 6 = \underline{1}$

There is **1 more** ⊛ than there are ⬇.

There is **1 fewer** ⬇ than there are ⊛.

Subtract to compare.

1. $5 - 3 = \underline{2}$

   $\underline{2}$ more

2. $6 - 4 = \underline{2}$

   $\underline{2}$ fewer

3. $4 - 1 = \underline{3}$

   $\underline{3}$ more

4. $7 - 3 = \underline{4}$

   $\underline{4}$ fewer

Lesson 43
CC.1.OA.8

1. How many fewer 🐦 are there?

   ● 1 fewer   ○ 7 fewer

   ○ 4 fewer   ○ 8 fewer

   $4 - 3 = \underline{}$

2. How many more ☕ are there?

   ○ 8 more   ● 4 more

   ○ 6 more   ○ 2 more

   $6 - 2 = \underline{}$

PROBLEM SOLVING REAL WORLD

Draw a picture to show the problem. Write a subtraction sentence to match your picture.

3. Jo has 4 golf clubs and 2 golf balls. How many fewer golf balls does Jo have?

   $\underline{4} - \underline{2} = \underline{2}$ $\underline{2}$ fewer

Lesson 44
COMMON CORE STANDARD CC.1.OA.8
Lesson Objective: Identify how many are left when subtracting all or 0.

Subtract All or Zero

When you subtract zero from a number, the difference is the number.

No ◯ are crossed out.

$4 - 0 = \underline{4}$

When you subtract a number from itself, the difference is zero.

All ◯ are crossed out.

$4 - 4 = \underline{0}$

Use ◯. Write the difference.

1. $3 - 3 = \underline{0}$

2. $5 - 0 = \underline{5}$

3. $2 - 0 = \underline{2}$

4. $1 - 1 = \underline{0}$

5. $6 - 0 = \underline{6}$

6. $4 - 4 = \underline{0}$

Lesson 44
CC.1.OA.8

1. Mary has 3 flowers. She gives 3 flowers to her mother. How many flowers does Mary have now?

   ● 0
   ○ 1
   ○ 2
   ○ 6

2. Carl has 7 grapes. He does not eat any grapes. How many grapes does Carl have left?

   ○ 17
   ● 7
   ○ 5
   ○ 0

3. What is the difference?

   $9 - 0 = \underline{}$

   ○ 0
   ○ 1
   ○ 8
   ● 9

4. What is the difference?

   $\underline{} = 6 - 6$

   ○ 12
   ○ 6
   ○ 3
   ● 0

5. Think about $5 - 5$ and $5 - 0$. Explain how they are alike and how they are different. Possible explanation: They both begin with 5. For $5 - 5$, you subtract 5, which leaves 0. For $5 - 0$, you do not subtract anything, which leaves 5.

Answer Key

Name _____ **Lesson 45**
COMMON CORE STANDARD CC.1.OA.8
Lesson Objective: Use related facts to
determine unknown numbers.

Algebra · Missing Numbers

Add or subtract to find the missing numbers.

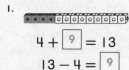

$6 + \boxed{5} = 11$

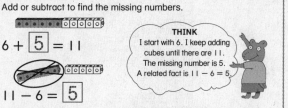

THINK
I start with 6. I keep adding
cubes until there are 11.
The missing number is 5.
A related fact is $11 - 6 = 5$.

$11 - 6 = \boxed{5}$

Use to find the missing numbers.
Write the numbers.

1.
$4 + \boxed{9} = 13$
$13 - 4 = \boxed{9}$

2.
$7 + \boxed{8} = 15$
$15 - 7 = \boxed{8}$

3.
$8 + \boxed{6} = 14$
$14 - 8 = \boxed{6}$

4.
$9 + \boxed{7} = 16$
$16 - 9 = \boxed{7}$

5.
$9 + \boxed{9} = 18$
$18 - 9 = \boxed{9}$

6.
$8 + \boxed{8} = 16$
$16 - 8 = \boxed{8}$

Name _____ **Lesson 45**
CC.1.OA.8

1. What is the missing number?

$5 + \boxed{} = 13$

$13 - 5 = \boxed{}$

○ 4
○ 5
● 8
○ 9

3. What is the missing number?

$6 + \boxed{} = 15$

$15 - 6 = \boxed{}$

○ 7
● 9
○ 11
○ 21

2. What is the missing number?

$4 + \boxed{} = 11$

$11 - 4 = \boxed{}$

○ 11
○ 10
○ 8
● 7

4. What is the missing number?

$8 + \boxed{} = 16$

○ 1
○ 6
● 8
○ 10

5. Write the missing number.

$17 - 8 = \underline{9}$

Name _____ **Lesson 46**
COMMON CORE STANDARD CC.1.OA.8
Lesson Objective: Use a related fact to
subtract.

Algebra · Use Related Facts

Find $11 - 6$.

Use counters to help you.

THINK
Start with 6. How
many do I add
to make 11?

$6 + \underline{5} = 11$

$11 - 6 = \underline{5}$

Use counters. Write the missing numbers.

1. Find $13 - 8$.

$8 + \underline{5} = 13$

$13 - 8 = \underline{5}$

2. Find $12 - 3$.

$3 + \underline{9} = 12$

$12 - 3 = \underline{9}$

Name _____ **Lesson 46**
CC.1.OA.8

1. What is the missing number?

$10 - 4 = \boxed{}$

$4 + \boxed{} = 10$

○ 3   ● 6
○ 4   ○ 7

3. What is the missing number?

$11 - 3 = \boxed{}$

$3 + \boxed{} = 11$

○ 7   ○ 9
● 8   ○ 11

2. What is the missing number?

$12 - 6 = \boxed{}$

$6 + \boxed{} = 12$

○ 4
○ 5
● 6
○ 9

4. Look at the shapes in the addition sentence. Which shape completes the related subtraction fact?

○   ●   ○   ○

5. Use the numbers 3, 9, and 12 to write 4 related facts.

$\underline{3} + \underline{9} = \underline{12}$ $\underline{12} - \underline{9} = \underline{3}$

$\underline{9} + \underline{3} = \underline{12}$ $\underline{12} - \underline{3} = \underline{9}$

Answer Key

Answer Key

Name _____ **Lesson 49**
COMMON CORE STANDARD CC.1.NBT.1
Lesson Objective: Read and write numerals to represent a number of 100 to 110 objects.

Model, Read, and Write
Numbers from 100 to 110

What is 10 tens and 2 more?

> Count by tens. Then count by ones.

10, 20, 30, 40, 50, 60, 70, 80, 90, __100__, __101__, __102__

10 tens and 2 more = __102__

Use ▭ to model the number.
Write the number.

1. 10 tens and 3 more   __103__
2. 10 tens and 7 more   __107__
3. 10 tens and 6 more   __106__
4. 10 tens and 9 more   __109__

www.harcourtschoolsupply.com
© Houghton Mifflin Harcourt Publishing Company
97
Core Standards for Math, Grade 1

Name _____ **Lesson 49**
CC.1.NBT.1

1. What number does the model show?
   13   93   ●103   113

2. Which number has 10 tens and 5 more?
   115   ●105   95   15

3. Which number has 10 tens and 9 ones?
   ●109   108   106   91

PROBLEM SOLVING REAL WORLD

4. Solve to find the number of pens.

THINK
= 1 pen
= 10 pens

There are __104__ pens.

www.harcourtschoolsupply.com
© Houghton Mifflin Harcourt Publishing Company
98
Core Standards for Math, Grade 1

Name _____ **Lesson 50**
COMMON CORE STANDARD CC.1.NBT.1
Lesson Objective: Read and write numerals to represent a number of 110 to 120 objects.

Model, Read, and Write
Numbers from 110 to 120

What is the number?

> Count by tens. Then count by ones.

10 20 30 40 50 60 70 80 90 100 110 111 112 113

The number is __113__.

Use ▭ to model the number.
Write the number.

1. __114__
2. __111__
3. __116__
4. __118__

www.harcourtschoolsupply.com
© Houghton Mifflin Harcourt Publishing Company
99
Core Standards for Math, Grade 1

Name _____ **Lesson 50**
CC.1.NBT.1

1. What number does the model show?
   15   105   111   ●115

2. Which number means the same as 12 tens?
   ●120   112   110   102

3. Which number means the same as 11 tens and 3 ones?
   103   111   ●113   114

PROBLEM SOLVING REAL WORLD

Choose a way to solve. Draw or write to explain.

4. Dave collects rocks. He makes 12 groups of 10 rocks and has none left over. How many rocks does Dave have?   __120__ rocks

www.harcourtschoolsupply.com
© Houghton Mifflin Harcourt Publishing Company
100
Core Standards for Math, Grade 1

---

www.harcourtschoolsupply.com
© Houghton Mifflin Harcourt Publishing Company
225
Core Standards for Math, Grade 1

Answer Key

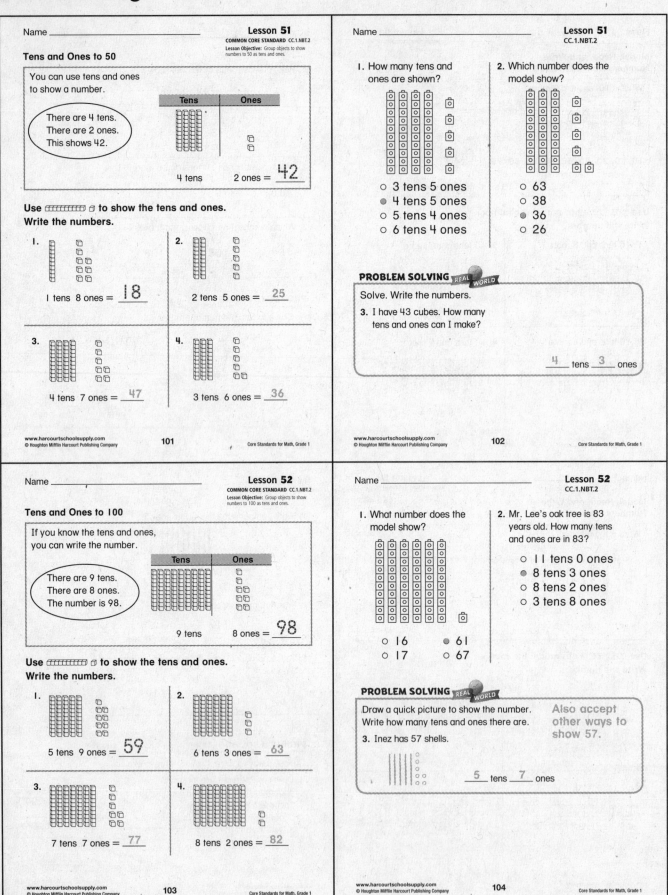

Name _____ **Lesson 51**
COMMON CORE STANDARD CC.1.NBT.2
Lesson Objective: Group objects to show
numbers to 50 as tens and ones.

Tens and Ones to 50

You can use tens and ones
to show a number.

Tens	Ones

There are 4 tens.
There are 2 ones.
This shows 42.

4 tens   2 ones = **42**

Use ⬚⬚⬚ **to show the tens and ones.**
Write the numbers.

1. 1 tens 8 ones = **18**

2. 2 tens 5 ones = **25**

3. 4 tens 7 ones = **47**

4. 3 tens 6 ones = **36**

1. How many tens and
ones are shown?

○ 3 tens 5 ones
● 4 tens 5 ones
○ 5 tens 4 ones
○ 6 tens 4 ones

2. Which number does the
model show?

○ 63
○ 38
● 36
○ 26

PROBLEM SOLVING REAL WORLD

Solve. Write the numbers.

3. I have 43 cubes. How many
tens and ones can I make?

4 tens **3** ones

Name _____ **Lesson 52**
COMMON CORE STANDARD CC.1.NBT.2
Lesson Objective: Group objects to show
numbers to 100 as tens and ones.

Tens and Ones to 100

If you know the tens and ones,
you can write the number.

Tens	Ones

There are 9 tens.
There are 8 ones.
The number is 98.

9 tens   8 ones = **98**

Use ⬚⬚⬚ **to show the tens and ones.**
Write the numbers.

1. 5 tens 9 ones = **59**

2. 6 tens 3 ones = **63**

3. 7 tens 7 ones = **77**

4. 8 tens 2 ones = **82**

1. What number does the
model show?

○ 16   ● 61
○ 17   ○ 67

2. Mr. Lee's oak tree is 83
years old. How many tens
and ones are in 83?

○ 11 tens 0 ones
● 8 tens 3 ones
○ 8 tens 2 ones
○ 3 tens 8 ones

PROBLEM SOLVING REAL WORLD

Draw a quick picture to show the number.
Write how many tens and ones there are.

3. Inez has 57 shells.

*Also accept
other ways to
show 57.*

5 tens **7** ones

Lesson 53

COMMON CORE STANDARD CC.1.NBT.2a
Lesson Objective: Solve problems using the strategy *make a model.*

Name _____

Problem Solving • Show Numbers in Different Ways

How can you show the number 34 two different ways?

Unlock the Problem

What do I need to find?	What information do I need to use?
two different ways to show a number	The number is _34_.

Show how to solve the problem.

> **THINK**
> You can trade 1 ten for 10 ones.

First Way		**Second Way**	
Tens	Ones	Tens	Ones

1. Use ▭ to show 26 two different ways. Draw both ways.

Possible answers: 2 tens 6 ones, 1 ten 16 ones, or 26 ones

Tens	Ones	Tens	Ones

Lesson 53

CC.1.NBT.2a

Name _____

1. Which is a different way to show the same number?

○   ●   ○   ○

2. Which number is the same as 3 tens and 22 ones?

23   32   42   52
○   ○   ○   ●

3. Which number is the same as 5 tens and 6 ones?

46   55   56   66
○   ○   ●   ○

4. Think of a number greater than 30. Your number should have two different digits. Write your number. Then make quick pictures to show your number three ways.

Possible answer shown. Also accept other ways to show 34.

First way   Second way   Third way

My number is _34_.

Lesson 54

COMMON CORE STANDARD CC.1.NBT.2b
Lesson Objective: Use models and write to represent equivalent forms of ten and ones.

Name _____

Understand Ten and Ones

You can use ▭ to show ten and some ones.
You can write ten and ones in different ways.

_1_ ten _2_ ones
$10 + 2$
12

Use the model. Write the number three different ways.

1. _1_ ten _3_ ones
$10 + 3$
13

2. _1_ ten _4_ ones
$10 + 4$
14

3. _1_ ten _7_ ones
$10 + 7$
17

Lesson 54

CC.1.NBT.2b

Name _____

1. Which shows the same number?

● $10 + 4$ ○ 10
○ $10 + 3$ ○ $10 - 4$

2. Look at the model. Which is **not** a way to write the number?

○ 1 ten 6 ones
○ $10 + 6$
○ 16
● 61

3. Which number means the same as 1 ten 9 ones?

109   91   19   16
○   ○   ●   ○

4. Pam has 8 ones. Bo has 3 ones. They put all their ones together. What number do they make?

5   11   12   83
○   ●   ○   ○

5. Use the model. Write the number three different ways.

_1_ ten _5_ ones
$10 + 5$
15

Answer Key

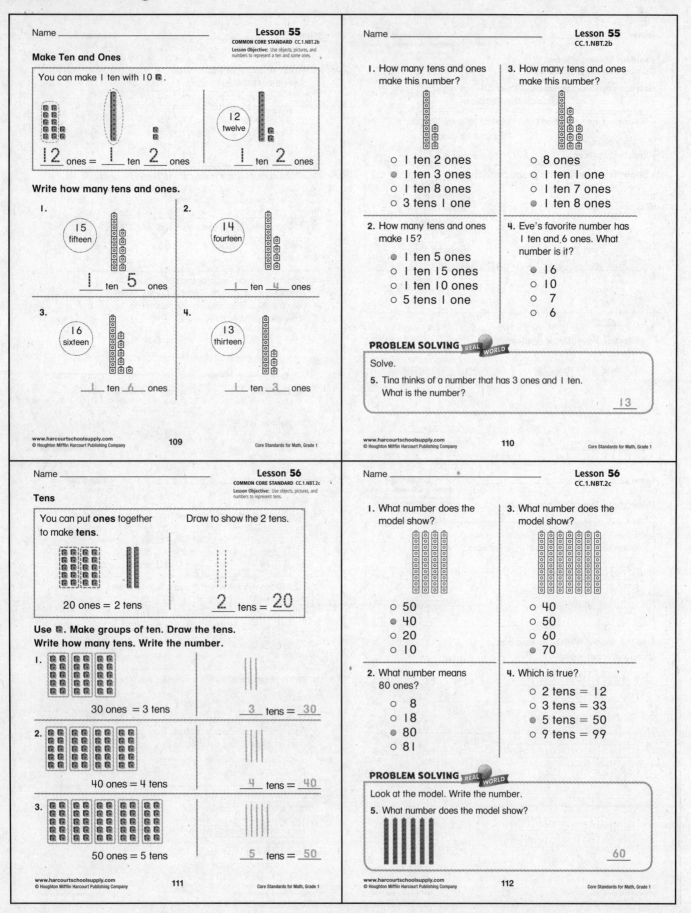

Name _____

Make Ten and Ones

You can make 1 ten with 10 🔲.

12 twelve

__12__ ones = __1__ ten __2__ ones

__1__ ten __2__ ones

Write how many tens and ones.

1. **15** fifteen
__1__ ten __5__ ones

2. **14** fourteen
__1__ ten __4__ ones

3. **16** sixteen
__1__ ten __6__ ones

4. **13** thirteen
__1__ ten __3__ ones

Name _____

1. How many tens and ones make this number?
   - ○ 1 ten 2 ones
   - ● 1 ten 3 ones
   - ○ 1 ten 8 ones
   - ○ 3 tens 1 one

2. How many tens and ones make 15?
   - ● 1 ten 5 ones
   - ○ 1 ten 15 ones
   - ○ 1 ten 10 ones
   - ○ 5 tens 1 one

3. How many tens and ones make this number?
   - ○ 8 ones
   - ○ 1 ten 1 one
   - ○ 1 ten 7 ones
   - ● 1 ten 8 ones

4. Eve's favorite number has 1 ten and 6 ones. What number is it?
   - ● 16
   - ○ 10
   - ○ 7
   - ○ 6

PROBLEM SOLVING REAL WORLD

Solve.

5. Tina thinks of a number that has 3 ones and 1 ten. What is the number?

__13__

Name _____

Tens

You can put **ones** together to make **tens**.

20 ones = 2 tens

Draw to show the 2 tens.

__2__ tens = __20__

Use 🔲. Make groups of ten. Draw the tens.
Write how many tens. Write the number.

1. 30 ones = 3 tens
__3__ tens = __30__

2. 40 ones = 4 tens
__4__ tens = __40__

3. 50 ones = 5 tens
__5__ tens = __50__

Name _____

1. What number does the model show?
   - ○ 50
   - ● 40
   - ○ 20
   - ○ 10

2. What number means 80 ones?
   - ○ 8
   - ○ 18
   - ● 80
   - ○ 81

3. What number does the model show?
   - ○ 40
   - ○ 50
   - ○ 60
   - ● 70

4. Which is true?
   - ○ 2 tens = 12
   - ○ 3 tens = 33
   - ● 5 tens = 50
   - ○ 9 tens = 99

PROBLEM SOLVING REAL WORLD

Look at the model. Write the number.

5. What number does the model show?

__60__

Answer Key

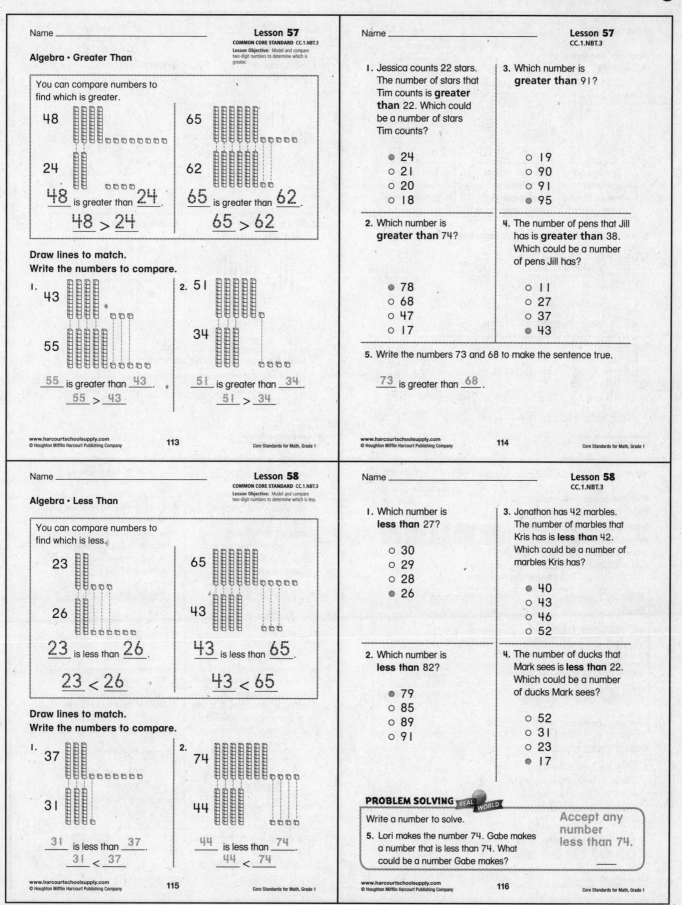

Name _____ **Lesson 57**
COMMON CORE STANDARD CC.1.NBT.3
Lesson Objective: Model and compare two-digit numbers to determine which is greater.

Algebra • Greater Than

You can compare numbers to find which is greater.

48

24

48 is greater than **24**.

48 > 24

65

62

65 is greater than **62**.

65 > 62

Draw lines to match.
Write the numbers to compare.

1. 43

   55

   55 is greater than **43**.

   55 > 43

2. 51

   34

   51 is greater than **34**.

   51 > 34

www.harcourtschoolsupply.com
© Houghton Mifflin Harcourt Publishing Company
113
Core Standards for Math, Grade 1

Name _____ **Lesson 57**
CC.1.NBT.3

1. Jessica counts 22 stars. The number of stars that Tim counts is **greater than** 22. Which could be a number of stars Tim counts?

   ● 24
   ○ 21
   ○ 20
   ○ 18

2. Which number is **greater than** 74?

   ● 78
   ○ 68
   ○ 47
   ○ 17

3. Which number is **greater than** 91?

   ○ 19
   ○ 90
   ○ 91
   ● 95

4. The number of pens that Jill has is **greater than** 38. Which could be a number of pens Jill has?

   ○ 11
   ○ 27
   ○ 37
   ● 43

5. Write the numbers 73 and 68 to make the sentence true.

   73 is greater than **68**.

www.harcourtschoolsupply.com
© Houghton Mifflin Harcourt Publishing Company
114
Core Standards for Math, Grade 1

Name _____ **Lesson 58**
COMMON CORE STANDARD CC.1.NBT.3
Lesson Objective: Model and compare two-digit numbers to determine which is less.

Algebra • Less Than

You can compare numbers to find which is less.

23

26

23 is less than **26**.

23 < 26

65

43

43 is less than **65**.

43 < 65

Draw lines to match.
Write the numbers to compare.

1. 37

   31

   31 is less than **37**.

   31 < 37

2. 74

   44

   44 is less than **74**.

   44 < 74

www.harcourtschoolsupply.com
© Houghton Mifflin Harcourt Publishing Company
115
Core Standards for Math, Grade 1

Name _____ **Lesson 58**
CC.1.NBT.3

1. Which number is **less than** 27?

   ○ 30
   ○ 29
   ○ 28
   ● 26

2. Which number is **less than** 82?

   ● 79
   ○ 85
   ○ 89
   ○ 91

3. Jonathon has 42 marbles. The number of marbles that Kris has is **less than** 42. Which could be a number of marbles Kris has?

   ● 40
   ○ 43
   ○ 46
   ○ 52

4. The number of ducks that Mark sees is **less than** 22. Which could be a number of ducks Mark sees?

   ○ 52
   ○ 31
   ○ 23
   ● 17

PROBLEM SOLVING REAL WORLD

Write a number to solve.

5. Lori makes the number 74. Gabe makes a number that is less than 74. What could be a number Gabe makes?

   _____

   Accept any number less than 74.

www.harcourtschoolsupply.com
© Houghton Mifflin Harcourt Publishing Company
116
Core Standards for Math, Grade 1

Answer Key

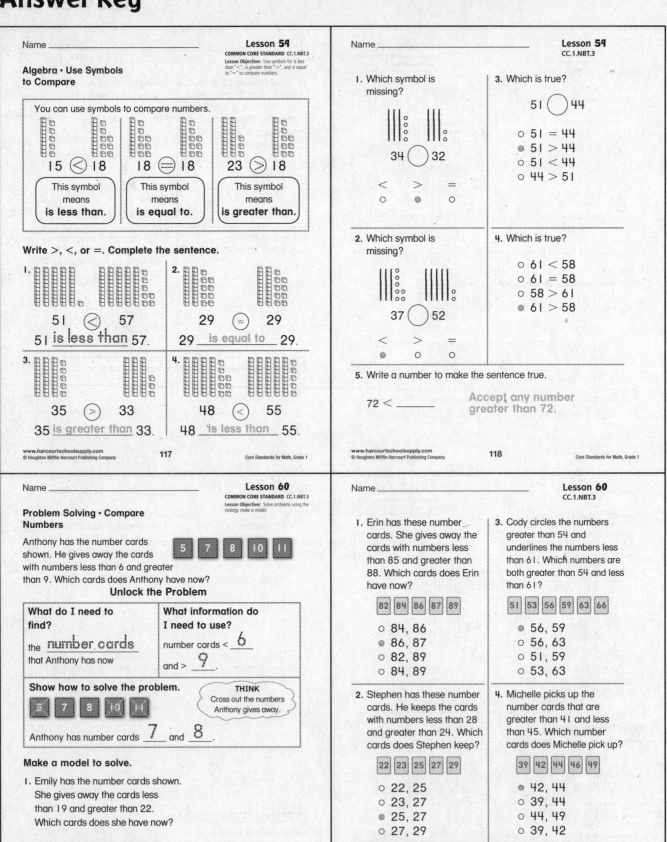

Name _____ **Lesson 59**
COMMON CORE STANDARD CC.1.NBT.3
Lesson Objective: Use symbols for *is less than* "<", *is greater than* ">", and *is equal to* "=" to compare numbers.

Algebra • Use Symbols to Compare

You can use symbols to compare numbers.

15 < 18   18 = 18   23 > 18

| This symbol means **is less than.** | This symbol means **is equal to.** | This symbol means **is greater than.** |

Write >, <, or =. Complete the sentence.

1. 51 (<) 57
51 _is less than_ 57.

2. 29 (=) 29
29 _is equal to_ 29.

3. 35 (>) 33
35 _is greater than_ 33.

4. 48 (<) 55
48 _is less than_ 55.

www.harcourtschoolsupply.com
© Houghton Mifflin Harcourt Publishing Company   117   Core Standards for Math, Grade 1

Name _____ **Lesson 59**
CC.1.NBT.3

1. Which symbol is missing?

34 ◯ 32

<   >   =
○   ●   ○

2. Which symbol is missing?

37 ◯ 52

<   >   =
●   ○   ○

3. Which is true?

51 ◯ 44

○ 51 = 44
● 51 > 44
○ 51 < 44
○ 44 > 51

4. Which is true?

○ 61 < 58
○ 61 = 58
○ 58 > 61
● 61 > 58

5. Write a number to make the sentence true.

72 < _____

Accept any number greater than 72.

www.harcourtschoolsupply.com
© Houghton Mifflin Harcourt Publishing Company   118   Core Standards for Math, Grade 1

Name _____ **Lesson 60**
COMMON CORE STANDARD CC.1.NBT.3
Lesson Objective: Solve problems using the strategy make a model.

Problem Solving • Compare Numbers

Anthony has the number cards shown. He gives away the cards with numbers less than 6 and greater than 9. Which cards does Anthony have now?

[5] [7] [8] [10] [11]

Unlock the Problem

| **What do I need to find?** | **What information do I need to use?** |
| the _number cards_ that Anthony has now | number cards < _6_ and > _9_. |

| **Show how to solve the problem.** | THINK Cross out the numbers Anthony gives away. |
| [5̶] [7] [8] [1̶0̶] [1̶1̶] | |

Anthony has number cards _7_ and _8_.

Make a model to solve.

1. Emily has the number cards shown. She gives away the cards less than 19 and greater than 22. Which cards does she have now?

[17] [18] [20] [21] [23]

Emily has _20_ and _21_.

www.harcourtschoolsupply.com
© Houghton Mifflin Harcourt Publishing Company   119   Core Standards for Math, Grade 1

Name _____ **Lesson 60**
CC.1.NBT.3

1. Erin has these number cards. She gives away the cards with numbers less than 85 and greater than 88. Which cards does Erin have now?

[82] [84] [86] [87] [89]

○ 84, 86
● 86, 87
○ 82, 89
○ 84, 89

2. Stephen has these number cards. He keeps the cards with numbers less than 28 and greater than 24. Which cards does Stephen keep?

[22] [23] [25] [27] [29]

○ 22, 25
○ 23, 27
● 25, 27
○ 27, 29

3. Cody circles the numbers greater than 54 and underlines the numbers less than 61. Which numbers are both greater than 54 and less than 61?

[51] [53] [56] [59] [63] [66]

● 56, 59
○ 56, 63
○ 51, 59
○ 53, 63

4. Michelle picks up the number cards that are greater than 41 and less than 45. Which number cards does Michelle pick up?

[39] [42] [44] [46] [49]

● 42, 44
○ 39, 44
○ 44, 49
○ 39, 42

5. Sue crossed out the numbers that are less than 91 and greater than 96. Circle the number that is left.

[90] (95) [97] [98] [99]

www.harcourtschoolsupply.com
© Houghton Mifflin Harcourt Publishing Company   120   Core Standards for Math, Grade 1

Answer Key

Name _____   **Lesson 61**
COMMON CORE STANDARD CC.1.NBT.4
Lesson Objective: Draw a model to add tens.

Add Tens

What is 10 + 30?

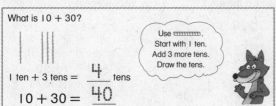

Use ▭▭▭.
Start with 1 ten.
Add 3 more tens.
Draw the tens.

1 ten + 3 tens = __4__ tens

10 + 30 = __40__

Use ▭▭▭. Draw to show tens.
Write how many tens. Write the sum.

1.
1 ten + 8 tens = __9__ tens
10 + 80 = __90__

2.
4 tens + 3 tens = __7__ tens
40 + 30 = __70__

3.
2 tens + 6 tens = __8__ tens
20 + 60 = __80__

4.
5 tens + 3 tens = __8__ tens
50 + 30 = __80__

Name _____   **Lesson 61**
CC.1.NBT.4

1. How many tens are
in the sum?

50 + 10 = 60

- ○ 1 ten
- ○ 5 tens
- ● 6 tens
- ○ 7 tens

2. How many tens are
in the sum?

20 + 60 = 80

- ○ 2 tens
- ○ 6 tens
- ○ 7 tens
- ● 8 tens

3. What is the sum?

70 + 20 = _____

- ○ 9
- ○ 50
- ○ 80
- ● 90

4. What is the sum?

30 + 40 = _____

- ○ 7
- ○ 10
- ● 70
- ○ 80

5. Draw groups of tens you can add to get a sum of 70.
Write the number sentence.
Check that children's drawings match their
numbers. Possible answers: 10 + 60 = 70, 20
+ 50 = 70, 30 + 40 = 70

Name _____   **Lesson 62**
COMMON CORE STANDARD CC.1.NBT.4
Lesson Objective: Use a hundred chart to
find sums.

Use a Hundred Chart to Add

You can count on to add on a
hundred chart.

Start at 21. Move right to count
on 3 ones. Count
22, **23**, **24**
21 + 3 = **24**

Start at 68. Move down to
count on 3 tens. Count
78, **88**, **98**
68 + 30 = **98**

Use the hundred chart to add.
Count on by ones.

1. 46 + 2 = __48__   2. 63 + 3 = __66__

Count on by tens.

3. 52 + 30 = __82__   4. 23 + 40 = __63__

Name _____   **Lesson 62**
CC.1.NBT.4

Use the hundred chart for 1–3.

1	2	3	4	5	6	7	8	9	10
11	12	13	14	15	16	17	18	19	20
21	22	23	24	25	26	27	28	29	30
31	32	33	34	35	36	37	38	39	40
41	42	43	44	45	46	47	48	49	50
51	52	53	54	55	56	57	58	59	60
61	62	63	64	65	66	67	68	69	70
71	72	73	74	75	76	77	78	79	80
81	82	83	84	85	86	87	88	89	90
91	92	93	94	95	96	97	98	99	100

2. Use the hundred chart to
add. Count on by tens.

67 + 30 = _____

- ● 97   ○ 87
- ○ 70   ○ 37

1. Use the hundred chart to
add. Count on by ones.

45 + 4 = _____

- ○ 38   ● 49
- ○ 48   ○ 59

3. Use the hundred chart to
add. Count on by tens.

20 + 51 = _____

- ● 71   ○ 31
- ○ 70   ○ 30

4. Add. Show your work on the
hundred chart.

23 + 40 + 10 = __73__

Check children's work.

Answer Key

Name _____

Lesson 63
COMMON CORE STANDARD CC.1.NBT.4
Lesson Objective: Use concrete models to add ones or tens to a two-digit number.

Use Models to Add

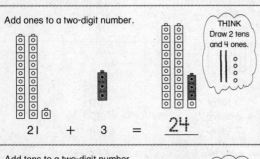

Add ones to a two-digit number.

THINK
Draw 2 tens and 4 ones.

21 + 3 = **24**

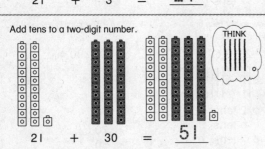

Add tens to a two-digit number.

THINK

21 + 30 = **51**

Use . Draw to show how to add the ones or tens. Write the sum.

Check children's drawings.

1. 15 + 2 = __17__   2. 15 + 20 = __35__

Name _____

Lesson 63
CC.1.NBT.4

1. What is the sum?

35 + 3 = _____

○ 33   ● 38
○ 37   ○ 43

3. What is the sum?

22 + 5 = _____

○ 24   ○ 52
● 27   ○ 57

2. What is the sum?

64 + 20 = _____

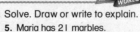

○ 66   ● 84
○ 74   ○ 86

4. What is the sum?

35 + 40 = _____

○ 39   ● 75
○ 65   ○ 79

PROBLEM SOLVING REAL WORLD

Solve. Draw or write to explain.

5. Maria has 21 marbles. She buys a bag of 20 marbles. How many marbles does Maria have now?

Check children's explanation.

21 + 20 = 41

__41__ marbles

Name _____

Lesson 64
COMMON CORE STANDARD CC.1.NBT.4
Lesson Objective: Make a ten to add a two-digit number and a one-digit number.

Make Ten to Add

What is 17 + 5?

Step 1
Use .
Show 17.
Use ○.
Show 5.

Step 2
Make a ten.

Step 3 Add.

20 + 2 = **22**

So, 17 + 5 = **22**.

Draw to show how you make a ten. Find the sum.

1. What is 16 + 8?

20 + **4** = **24**

So, 16 + 8 = **24**.

Name _____

Lesson 64
CC.1.NBT.4

1. Make a ten to find the sum.

34 + 7 = _____

○ 31   ○ 42
● 41   ○ 46

3. What is 28 + 4?

○ 24
○ 30
● 32
○ 34

2. Make a ten to find the sum.

52 + 9 = _____

○ 51   ○ 62
● 61   ○ 72

4. What is 79 + 6?

○ 84
● 85
○ 86
○ 87

PROBLEM SOLVING REAL WORLD

Choose a way to solve. Draw or write to show your work.

5. Debbie has 27 markers. Sal has 9 markers. How many markers do they have?

Check children's work.

27 + 9 = 36

__36__ markers

Answer Key

Name _____

Lesson 65
COMMON CORE STANDARD CC.1.NBT.4
Lesson Objective: Use tens and ones to add two-digit numbers.

Use Place Value to Add

You can use tens and ones to help you add.

Add 25 and 22.

Show 25. →

Show 22. →

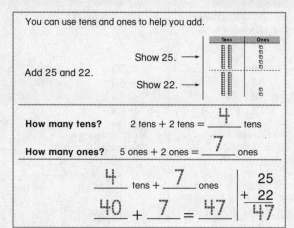

How many tens?   2 tens + 2 tens = __4__ tens

How many ones?   5 ones + 2 ones = __7__ ones

__4__ tens + __7__ ones

__40__ + __7__ = __47__

$\begin{array}{r} 25 \\ + 22 \\ \hline 47 \end{array}$

Use tens and ones to add.

1. Add 34 and 42.

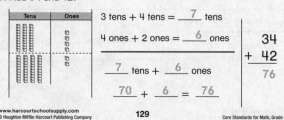

3 tens + 4 tens = __7__ tens

4 ones + 2 ones = __6__ ones

__7__ tens + __6__ ones

__70__ + __6__ = __76__

$\begin{array}{r} 34 \\ + 42 \\ \hline 76 \end{array}$

Name _____

Lesson 65
CC.1.NBT.4

1. Use tens and ones to add.

$\begin{array}{r} 42 \quad \text{4 tens + 2 ones} \\ + 15 \quad \text{1 ten + 5 ones} \end{array}$

○ 27 = 2 tens + 7 ones
○ 37 = 3 tens + 7 ones
○ 47 = 4 tens + 7 ones
◉ 57 = 5 tens + 7 ones

3. How many tens and ones are in the sum?

$\begin{array}{r} 81 \\ + 13 \end{array}$

○ 7 tens + 2 ones
○ 7 tens + 4 ones
○ 9 tens + 3 ones
◉ 9 tens + 4 ones

2. Use tens and ones to add.

$\begin{array}{r} 27 \quad \text{2 tens + 7 ones} \\ + 31 \quad \text{3 tens + 1 one} \end{array}$

◉ 58 = 5 tens + 8 ones
○ 68 = 6 tens + 8 ones
○ 95 = 9 tens + 5 ones
○ 50 = 5 tens + 0 ones

4. How many tens and ones are in the sum?

$\begin{array}{r} 45 \\ + 21 \end{array}$

○ 6 tens + 1 one
○ 6 tens + 5 ones
◉ 6 tens + 6 ones
○ 7 tens + 1 one

5. Use tens and ones to add.

37 + 15

37 + __3__ + 12

__40__ + 12 = __52__

So, 37 + 15 = __52__

Name _____

Lesson 66
COMMON CORE STANDARD CC.1.NBT.4
Lesson Objective: Solve and explain two-digit addition word problems using the strategy draw a picture.

Problem Solving • Addition Word Problems

Morgan plants 17 seeds.
Amy plants 8 seeds.
How many seeds do they plant?

Unlock the Problem

What do I need to find?

how many __seeds__ they plant

What information do I need to use?

Morgan plants __17__ seeds.

Amy plants __8__ seeds.

Show how to solve the problem.

count on ones
~~make a ten~~
add tens and ones

__25__ seeds.

Draw to solve. Circle your reasoning.

1. Edward buys 24 tomato plants.
He buys 15 pepper plants.
How many plants does he buy?

count on tens
make a ten
(add tens and ones)

__39__ plants

Check children's work.

Name _____

Lesson 66
CC.1.NBT.4

1. Lin picks 12 apples.
Pete picks 7 apples.
Which number sentence shows how many apples they pick?

○ 7 + 5 = 12
○ 7 + 7 = 14
○ 12 + 5 = 17
◉ 12 + 7 = 19

3. Paul finds 35 shells.
Then he finds 20 more shells. How many shells does Paul find?

○ 50
◉ 55
○ 60
○ 65

2. Jay has 41 trading cards.
Mel has 24 trading cards.
Which number sentence shows how many trading cards they have?

○ 24 + 17 = 41
○ 24 + 24 = 48
◉ 24 + 41 = 65
○ 41 + 17 = 58

4. Shondra uses 64 beads for a necklace. Then she uses 26 beads for another necklace. How many beads does Shondra use?

○ 38
○ 80
○ 82
◉ 90

5. Yuko recycles 17 bottles. Til recycles 8 bottles. How many bottles do they recycle?

__25__ bottles

Tell how you found your answer.

Possible explanation: I made a ten and added the rest of the ones.

Answer Key

Name _____

Lesson 67
COMMON CORE STANDARD CC.1.NBT.5
Lesson Objective: Identify numbers that are
10 less or 10 more than a given number.

10 Less, 10 More

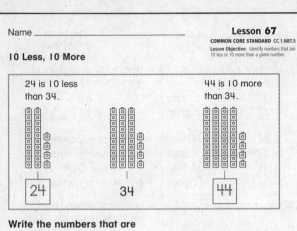

24 is 10 less than 34.

44 is 10 more than 34.

24   34   44

**Write the numbers that are
10 less and 10 more.**

1.

25   35   45

2.

12   22   32

Name _____

Lesson 67
CC.1.NBT.5

1. Ted has 18 marbles. Jamie has 10 more marbles than Ted. How many marbles does Jamie have?

○ 38
○ 37
● 28
○ 8

3. What number is 10 more than 63?

○ 53
○ 63
● 73
○ 83

2. What number is 10 less than 52?

○ 62
○ 52
○ 51
● 42

4. What numbers are 10 less and 10 more?

○ 42, 52
● 52, 72
○ 52, 62
○ 60, 70

5. Draw a quick picture to show the number that is 10 less than 87. Write the number.

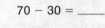

77

Name _____

Lesson 68
COMMON CORE STANDARD CC.1.NBT.6
Lesson Objective: Draw a model to subtract tens.

Subtract Tens

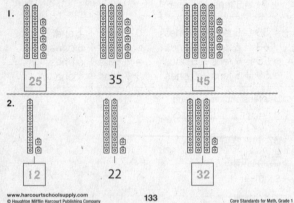

What is 60 − 40?

Use ▭. Show 6 tens. Take away 4 tens. 2 tens are left.

6 tens − 4 tens = __2__ tens

60 − 40 = __20__

**Use ▭. Draw to show tens.
Write how many tens. Write the difference.**

1.

7 tens − 4 tens = __3__ tens

70 − 40 = __30__

2.

9 tens − 5 tens = __4__ tens

90 − 50 = __40__

3.

5 tens − 2 tens = __3__ tens

50 − 20 = __30__

4.

8 tens − 7 tens = __1__ ten

80 − 70 = __10__

Name _____

Lesson 68
CC.1.NBT.6

1. How many tens are in the difference?

60 − 10 = 50

○ 1 ten
○ 4 tens
● 5 tens
○ 6 tens

3. What is the difference?

70 − 30 = _____

○ 10
○ 20
○ 30
● 40

2. How many tens are in the difference?

80 − 40 = 40

○ 8 tens
○ 6 tens
○ 5 tens
● 4 tens

4. What is the difference?

40 − 20 = _____

○ 60
○ 40
● 20
○ 10

5. Kim has 50 strawberries. She gives some to Andy. She has 30 strawberries left. How many strawberries did Kim give to Andy?

__20__ strawberries

Answer Key

Name _____

Lesson 69
COMMON CORE STANDARD CC.1.NBT.6
Lesson Objective: Add and subtract within 100, including continued practice with facts within 20.

Practice Addition and Subtraction

You can use models to add and subtract.

$13 + 5 = \underline{18}$

$90 - 60 = \underline{30}$

Add or subtract.

1. $33 + 6 = \underline{39}$	2. $10 + 10 = \underline{20}$	3. $15 - 8 = \underline{7}$
4. $6 + 7 = \underline{13}$	5. $54 + 23 = \underline{77}$	6. $71 + 8 = \underline{79}$
7. $5 + 5 = \underline{10}$	8. $8 - 8 = \underline{0}$	9. $16 + 3 = \underline{19}$
10. $55 + 12 = \underline{67}$	11. $9 - 7 = \underline{2}$	12. $30 - 10 = \underline{20}$

Name _____

Lesson 69
CC.1.NBT.6

1. Make a ten to find the sum.

$8 + 6 = \underline{\quad}$

$8 + 2 + 4$

$10 \quad + \quad 4$

- ● 14
- ○ 40
- ○ 41
- ○ 86

3. What is the sum?

$$\begin{array}{r} 33 \\ + 15 \\ \hline \end{array}$$

- ○ 42
- ○ 47
- ● 48
- ○ 58

2. What is the difference?

$60 - 40 = \underline{\quad}$

6 tens − 4 tens

- ○ 10
- ● 20
- ○ 30
- ○ 40

4. What is the difference?

$70 - 70 = \underline{\quad}$

- ● 0
- ○ 7
- ○ 10
- ○ 77

5. Write 3 ways to get a difference of 15.
Answers will vary. Possible answers shown.

$\underline{25} - \underline{10} = \underline{15}$

$\underline{21} - \underline{6} = \underline{15}$

$\underline{70} - \underline{55} = \underline{15}$

Name _____

Lesson 70
COMMON CORE STANDARD CC.1.MD.1
Lesson Objective: Order objects by length.

Order Length

You can put objects in order by length.

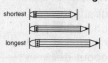

These pencils are in order from **shortest** to **longest**.

shortest

longest

These pencils are in order from **longest** to **shortest**.

longest

shortest

Draw three lines in order from **shortest** to **longest**.
Check children's drawings.

1. shortest

2.

3. longest

Draw three lines in order from **longest** to **shortest**.
Check children's drawings.

4. longest

5.

6. shortest

Name _____

Lesson 70
CC.1.MD.1

1. Which ribbon is the shortest?

- ○
- ○
- ●
- ○

3. Which pencil is the longest?

- ○
- ○
- ○
- ●

2. Which string is the shortest?

- ●
- ○
- ○
- ○

4. Which cube train is the longest?

- ○
- ○
- ○
- ●

PROBLEM SOLVING REAL WORLD

Solve.

5. Fred has the shortest toothbrush in the bathroom. Circle Fred's toothbrush.

Answer Key

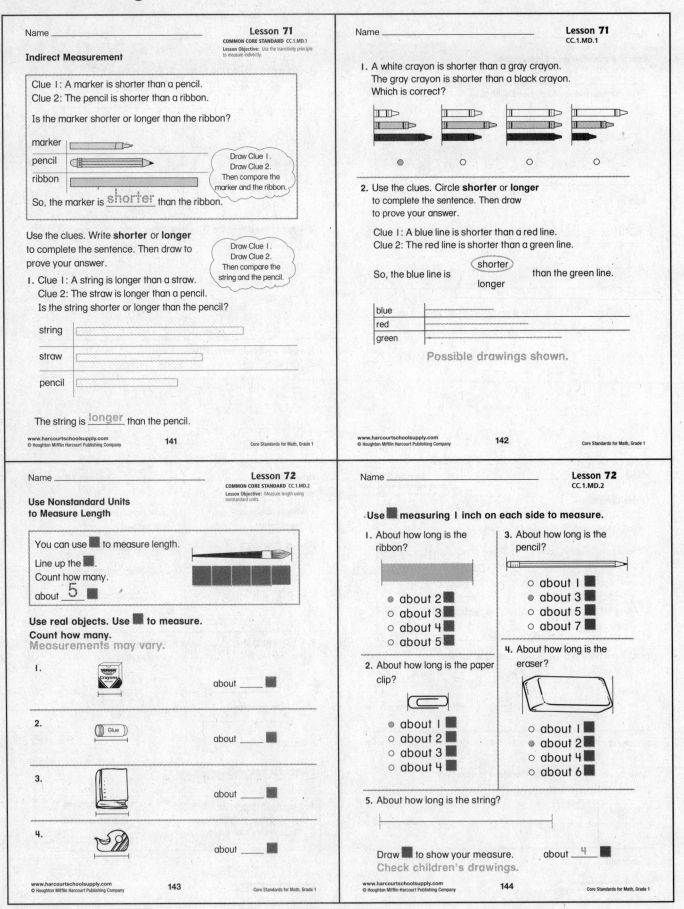

Name _____

Lesson 71
COMMON CORE STANDARD CC.1.MD.1
Lesson Objective: Use the transitivity principle to measure indirectly.

Indirect Measurement

Clue 1: A marker is shorter than a pencil.
Clue 2: The pencil is shorter than a ribbon.

Is the marker shorter or longer than the ribbon?

marker

pencil

ribbon

*Draw Clue 1.
Draw Clue 2.
Then compare the marker and the ribbon.*

So, the marker is **shorter** than the ribbon.

Use the clues. Write **shorter** or **longer**
to complete the sentence. Then draw to
prove your answer.

*Draw Clue 1.
Draw Clue 2.
Then compare the string and the pencil.*

1. Clue 1: A string is longer than a straw.
   Clue 2: The straw is longer than a pencil.
   Is the string shorter or longer than the pencil?

string

straw

pencil

The string is **longer** than the pencil.

---

1. A white crayon is shorter than a gray crayon.
   The gray crayon is shorter than a black crayon.
   Which is correct?

   ● ○ ○ ○

2. Use the clues. Circle **shorter** or **longer**
   to complete the sentence. Then draw
   to prove your answer.

   Clue 1: A blue line is shorter than a red line.
   Clue 2: The red line is shorter than a green line.

   So, the blue line is (**shorter** / longer) than the green line.

   blue
   red
   green

   Possible drawings shown.

Name _____

Lesson 72
COMMON CORE STANDARD CC.1.MD.2
Lesson Objective: Measure length using nonstandard units.

**Use Nonstandard Units
to Measure Length**

You can use ▓ to measure length.

Line up the ▓.
Count how many.
about __5__ ▓

Use real objects. Use ▓ to measure.
Count how many.
Measurements may vary.

1. Crayons   about ____ ▓

2. Glue   about ____ ▓

3.   about ____ ▓

4.   about ____ ▓

Use ▓ measuring 1 inch on each side to measure.

1. About how long is the
   ribbon?

   ● about 2 ▓
   ○ about 3 ▓
   ○ about 4 ▓
   ○ about 5 ▓

2. About how long is the paper
   clip?

   ● about 1 ▓
   ○ about 2 ▓
   ○ about 3 ▓
   ○ about 4 ▓

3. About how long is the
   pencil?

   ○ about 1 ▓
   ● about 3 ▓
   ○ about 5 ▓
   ○ about 7 ▓

4. About how long is the
   eraser?

   ○ about 1 ▓
   ● about 2 ▓
   ○ about 4 ▓
   ○ about 6 ▓

5. About how long is the string?

   Draw ▓ to show your measure.   about __4__ ▓
   Check children's drawings.

Lesson 73 — Page 145

Name _____

Lesson 73
COMMON CORE STANDARD CC.1.MD.2
Lesson Objective: Make a nonstandard measuring tool to measure length.

Make a Nonstandard Measuring Tool

About how long is the ribbon?
Count to measure.

_10_

Count on by ones.

about _15_ 🔗

Use real objects and the measuring tool you made. Measure.
Measurements may vary.

1. about _____ 🔗

2. about _____ 🔗

3. about _____ 🔗

Lesson 73 — Page 146

Name _____

Lesson 73
CC.1.MD.2

1. Joy measures her book with 🔗.
About how long is her book?
   - ○ about 3 🔗
   - ● about 6 🔗
   - ○ about 10 🔗
   - ○ about 15 🔗

2. Bo used this paper clip to measure a line.

Which line is about 3 paper clips long?
   - ○
   - ●
   - ○
   - ○

3. Molly is measuring a paintbrush with paper clips.
Write two things she should do.

Possible answers: Line up the end of the first paper clip with the end of the object, and put paper clips close together.

Lesson 74 — Page 147

Name _____

Lesson 74
COMMON CORE STANDARD CC.1.MD.2
Lesson Objective: Solve measurement problems using the strategy *act it out.*

**Problem Solving •
Measure and Compare**

The gray ribbon is 3 🔗 long. The white ribbon is 4 🔗 long. The black ribbon is 1 🔗 longer than the white ribbon. Draw and color the length of the ribbons in order from **shortest** to **longest**.

What do I need to find?	What information do I need to use?
order the ribbons from _shortest_ to _longest_	_Measure_ the ribbons using paper clips.

Show how to solve the problem.

shortest

1 2 3 about _3_ 🔗

1 2 3 4 about _4_ 🔗

longest

1 2 3 4 5 about _5_ 🔗

1. The _gray_ ribbon is the shortest ribbon.

2. The _black_ ribbon is the longest ribbon.

Lesson 74 — Page 148

Name _____

Lesson 74
CC.1.MD.2

1. The red book is about 9 🔗 long. The blue book is 2 🔗 shorter than the red book. The green book is 1 🔗 shorter than the blue book. Which lists the book colors in order from **shortest** to **longest**?
   - ○ red, blue, green
   - ○ blue, green, red
   - ● green, blue, red
   - ○ green, red, blue

2. The pink box is about 8 🔗 long. The blue box is 2 🔗 longer than the pink box. The gold box is 3 🔗 shorter than the pink box. Which lists the box colors in order from **longest** to **shortest**?
   - ○ gold, pink, blue
   - ○ blue, gold, pink
   - ○ pink, gold, blue
   - ● blue, pink, gold

PROBLEM SOLVING REAL WORLD

3. Sandy has a ribbon about 4 🔗 long. She cut a new ribbon 2 🔗 longer. Measure and draw the two ribbons.

The new ribbon is about _6_ 🔗 long.

Answer Key

Lesson 75
COMMON CORE STANDARD CC.1.MD.3
Lesson Objective: Write times to the hour shown on analog clocks.

Time to the Hour

Look at the hour hand.

The hour hand points to the __8__.

It is __8:00__.

Look at where the hour hand points. Write the time.

1. The hour hand points to the __2__.

   It is __2:00__.

2. The hour hand points to the __11__.

   It is __11:00__.

3. __9:00__

4. __6:00__

5. __4:00__

---

1. Look at the hour hand. What is the time?

   ○ 5:00   ○ 3:00
   ● 4:00   ○ 2:00

2. Look at the hour hand. What is the time?

   ● 11:00   ○ 8:00
   ○ 10:00   ○ 1:00

3. Look at the hour hand. What is the time?

   ○ 2:00   ● 6:00
   ○ 5:00   ○ 12:00

4. Look at the hour hand. What is the time?

   ○ 1:00   ● 7:00
   ○ 6:00   ○ 8:00

5. Look at where the hour hand points. Write the time.

   __9:00__

Lesson 76
COMMON CORE STANDARD CC.1.MD.3
Lesson Objective: Write times to the half hour shown on analog clocks.

Time to the Half Hour

The hour hand points halfway between

the __9__ and the __10__.

It is __half past 9:00__.

Look at where the hour hand points. Write the time.

1. The hour hand points halfway between

   the __6__ and the __7__.

   It is __half past 6:00__.

2. The hour hand points halfway between

   the __4__ and the __5__.

   It is __half past 4:00__.

3. __half past 2:00__

4. __half past 11:00__

5. __half past 5:00__

---

1. Look at the hour hand. What is the time?

   ○ 3:00
   ● half past 3:00
   ○ 4:00
   ○ half past 4:00

2. Look at the hour hand. What is the time?

   ○ half past 5:00
   ○ 5:00
   ● half past 4:00
   ○ 4:00

3. Look at the hour hand. What is the time?

   ○ half past 10:00   ● half past 9:00
   ○ 10:00   ○ 9:00

4. Mindy woke up at 7:30. Leah ate lunch at 12:30. Write the name of the person whose activity matches the time.

   __Leah__

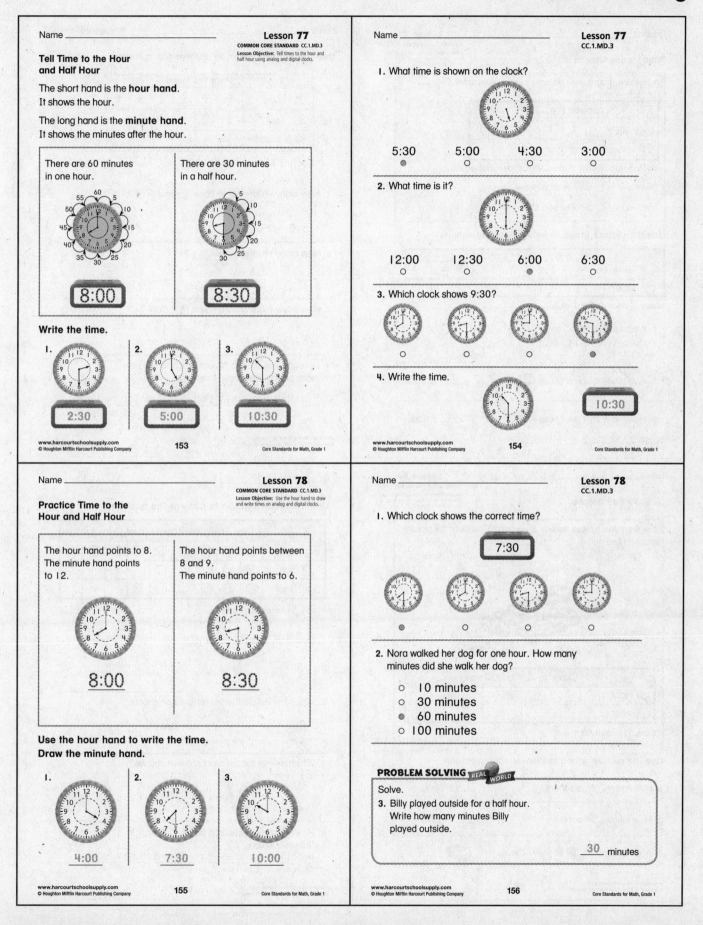

Name _____ **Lesson 77**
COMMON CORE STANDARD CC.1.MD.3
Lesson Objective: Tell times to the hour and half hour using analog and digital clocks.

Tell Time to the Hour and Half Hour

The short hand is the **hour hand**.
It shows the hour.

The long hand is the **minute hand**.
It shows the minutes after the hour.

There are 60 minutes in one hour.

8:00

There are 30 minutes in a half hour.

8:30

Write the time.

1. **2:30**

2. **5:00**

3. **10:30**

Name _____ **Lesson 77**
CC.1.MD.3

1. What time is shown on the clock?

5:30 ● 5:00 ○ 4:30 ○ 3:00 ○

2. What time is it?

12:00 ○ 12:30 ○ 6:00 ● 6:30 ○

3. Which clock shows 9:30?

○ ○ ○ ●

4. Write the time.

10:30

Name _____ **Lesson 78**
COMMON CORE STANDARD CC.1.MD.3
Lesson Objective: Use the hour hand to draw and write times on analog and digital clocks.

Practice Time to the Hour and Half Hour

The hour hand points to 8.
The minute hand points to 12.

8:00

The hour hand points between 8 and 9.
The minute hand points to 6.

8:30

Use the hour hand to write the time.
Draw the minute hand.

1. **4:00**

2. **7:30**

3. **10:00**

Name _____ **Lesson 78**
CC.1.MD.3

1. Which clock shows the correct time?

7:30

● ○ ○ ○

2. Nora walked her dog for one hour. How many minutes did she walk her dog?

○ 10 minutes
○ 30 minutes
● 60 minutes
○ 100 minutes

PROBLEM SOLVING REAL WORLD

Solve.

3. Billy played outside for a half hour. Write how many minutes Billy played outside.

_30_ minutes

Answer Key

Name _____   Lesson 79
COMMON CORE STANDARD CC.1.MD.4
Lesson Objective: Analyze and compare data shown in a picture graph where each symbol represents one.

Read Picture Graphs

A **picture graph** uses pictures to show how many. Count the ⚲ in each row.

Snack We Like					
🍎 apple	⚲	⚲	⚲	⚲	⚲
🥨 pretzel	⚲	⚲	⚲		

Each ⚲ stands for 1 child who chose that snack.

There are __5__ children who chose 🍎.

There are __3__ children who chose 🥨.

Use the picture graph to answer each question.

What We Ate for Lunch					
🥪 sandwich	⚲	⚲	⚲	⚲	⚲
🥫 soup	⚲	⚲			

Each ⚲ stands for 1 child.

1. Which lunch did more children choose? Circle.

2. How many children chose 🥪? __6__ children

3. How many children chose 🥫? __2__ children

Use the picture graph to answer the question.

Pets We Have						
🐕 dog	⚲	⚲	⚲	⚲	⚲	⚲
🐈 cat	⚲	⚲	⚲	⚲	⚲	
🐹 hamster	⚲	⚲				

Each ⚲ stands for 1 child.

1. How many children in all have 🐈 and 🐹?

   ○ 3   ● 7   ○ 4   ○ 11

2. How many children have 🐹?

   ● 2   ○ 4   ○ 5   ○ 6

3. How many more children have 🐕 than 🐈?

   ○ 11   ○ 6   ○ 5   ● 1

4. How can you use the picture graph to find how many pets in all? Show your work.

   Possible answer: I can count all the pictures in all the rows; 6 + 5 + 2 = 13 pets in all.

Name _____   Lesson 80
COMMON CORE STANDARD CC.1.MD.4
Lesson Objective: Make a picture graph where each symbol represents one and interpret the information.

Make Picture Graphs

Are there more black cars or white cars? Complete the picture graph to find out.

Cross out each car as you count.

Draw a ◯ in the graph to show each car.

Black and White Cars									
🚗 black	◯	◯	◯	◯	◯	◯			
🚗 white	◯	◯	◯	◯	◯	◯	◯	◯	◯

Each ◯ stands for 1 car.

Use the picture graph to answer each question.

1. How many 🚗 are there? __6__

2. How many 🚗 are there? __10__

3. Are there more 🚗 or 🚗? Circle.

Use the picture graph to answer the question.

Our Favorite Zoo Animal								
🐒 ape	☺	☺	☺	☺	☺	☺	☺	☺
🦁 lion	☺	☺	☺	☺	☺			
🦭 seal	☺	☺	☺	☺	☺	☺		

Each ☺ stands for 1 child.

1. How many children chose 🦁?

   3 ○   4 ○   6 ●   8 ○

2. Which animal did the fewest children choose?

   🐒 ○   🦁 ●   🦭 ○   🦒 ○

3. Which animal did the most children choose?

   🐒 ●   🦁 ○   🦭 ○   🦒 ○

4. How many more children chose 🐒 than 🦁? Show your work.

   8 children chose ape, 5 chose lion, so 3 more chose ape.

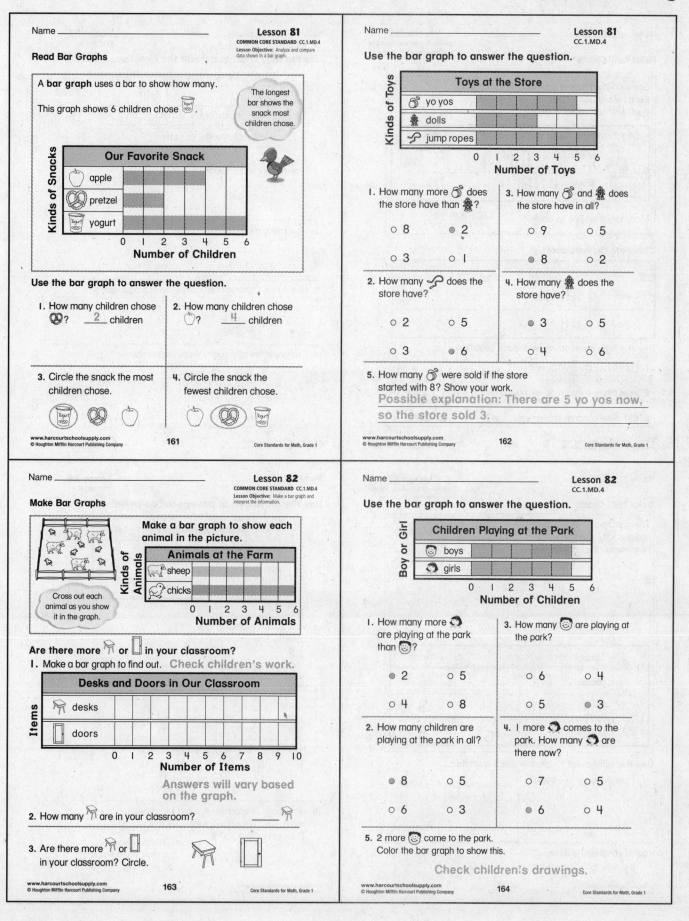

Name _____   Lesson **81**
COMMON CORE STANDARD CC.1.MD.4
Lesson Objective: Analyze and compare data shown in a bar graph.

Read Bar Graphs

A **bar graph** uses a bar to show how many.

This graph shows 6 children chose 🥛 .

The longest bar shows the snack most children chose.

Our Favorite Snack

Kinds of Snacks

apple
pretzel
yogurt

0 1 2 3 4 5 6
Number of Children

Use the bar graph to answer the question.

1. How many children chose 🥨 ? __2__ children

2. How many children chose 🍎 ? __4__ children

3. Circle the snack the most children chose.

4. Circle the snack the fewest children chose.

Name _____   Lesson **81**
CC.1.MD.4

Use the bar graph to answer the question.

Kinds of Toys

Toys at the Store

yo yos
dolls
jump ropes

0 1 2 3 4 5 6
Number of Toys

1. How many more 🪀 does the store have than 🧸 ?

○ 8   ● 2

○ 3   ○ 1

3. How many 🪀 and 🧸 does the store have in all?

○ 9   ○ 5

● 8   ○ 2

2. How many 〜 does the store have?

○ 2   ○ 5

○ 3   ● 6

4. How many 🧸 does the store have?

● 3   ○ 5

○ 4   ○ 6

5. How many 🪀 were sold if the store started with 8? Show your work.

Possible explanation: There are 5 yo yos now, so the store sold 3.

Name _____   Lesson **82**
COMMON CORE STANDARD CC.1.MD.4
Lesson Objective: Make a bar graph and interpret the information.

Make Bar Graphs

Make a bar graph to show each animal in the picture.

Kinds of Animals

Animals at the Farm

sheep
chicks

0 1 2 3 4 5 6
Number of Animals

Cross out each animal as you show it in the graph.

Are there more 🪑 or 🚪 in your classroom?

1. Make a bar graph to find out. Check children's work.

Items

Desks and Doors in Our Classroom

desks
doors

0 1 2 3 4 5 6 7 8 9 10
Number of Items

Answers will vary based on the graph.

2. How many 🪑 are in your classroom? _____

3. Are there more 🪑 or 🚪 in your classroom? Circle.

Name _____   Lesson **82**
CC.1.MD.4

Use the bar graph to answer the question.

Boy or Girl

Children Playing at the Park

boys
girls

0 1 2 3 4 5 6
Number of Children

1. How many more 👦 are playing at the park than 👧 ?

● 2   ○ 5

○ 4   ○ 8

3. How many 👦 are playing at the park?

○ 6   ○ 4

○ 5   ● 3

2. How many children are playing at the park in all?

● 8   ○ 5

○ 6   ○ 3

4. 1 more 👧 comes to the park. How many 👧 are there now?

○ 7   ○ 5

● 6   ○ 4

5. 2 more 👦 come to the park. Color the bar graph to show this.

Check children's drawings.

Answer Key

COMMON CORE STANDARD CC.1.MD.4
Lesson Objective: Analyze and compare
data shown in a tally chart.

Read Tally Charts

Some children named their favorite collections.
Each | stands for 1 child.
Each ЖЖ stands for 5 children.

Our Favorite Thing to Collect		Total
shells	|||| 1 2 3 4	4
stamps	ЖЖ || 5 6 7	7

More children like to collect ____stamps____.

Complete the tally chart.

Do you have a pet?		Total
yes	ЖЖ |||	8
no	ЖЖ	5

Use the tally chart to answer each question.

1. How many children have a pet? _____8_____ children

2. How many children do not have a pet? _____5_____ children

3. Did more children answer yes or no? _____yes_____

Use the tally chart to answer the question.

Our Favorite Lunch		Total
pizza	ЖЖ |||	
sandwich	||||	
spaghetti	|||	

1. How many children chose 🍕?

   2   3   4   5
   ○   ○   ●   ○

2. How many more children chose 🥪 than 🍝?

   1   3   4   7
   ●   ○   ○   ○

3. How many children in all chose their favorite lunch?

   16   15   12   11
   ○   ●   ○   ○

4. Complete the tally chart. Write the numbers.

Check children's charts: pizza 8,
sandwich 4; spaghetti 3.

COMMON CORE STANDARD CC.1.MD.4
Lesson Objective: Make a tally chart and
interpret the information.

Make Tally Charts

The picture shows shapes.
Make a tally chart to show
how many of each shape.

Cross out each shape as you count.

Shapes in the Picture		Total
circles	ЖЖ |	6
stars	|||	3
triangles	ЖЖ |||	8

Use the tally chart to answer each question.

1. How many ☆ are there?

2. How many more △ than ○ are there?

   _____3_____ ☆   _____2_____ more △

3. Which shape is there
the most of? Circle.
   ○   ☆   △⃝

Use the tally chart to answer the question.

Our Favorite Vegetable		Total
carrot	ЖЖ |	6
corn	ЖЖ ||||	9
tomato	ЖЖ	

1. How many children chose 🍅?

   2   5   6   9
   ○   ●   ○   ○

2. How many children chose 🌽 and 🥕?

   6   9   14   15
   ○   ○   ○   ●

3. How many more children chose 🥕 than 🍅?

   1   2   8   4
   ●   ○   ○   ○

4. How many children in all voted for a favorite
vegetable? Show the total in tally marks.
Then write the number.

   _____20_____ children in all.

Check that children
correctly make tally
marks for 20.

Answer Key

Name _____

Lesson 85
COMMON CORE STANDARD CC.1.MD.4
Lesson Objective: Solve problem situations using the strategy *make a graph.*

Problem Solving • Represent Data

Ava has these beads to make a bracelet.
How can you find how many beads she has?

Unlock the Problem

What do I need to find?	**What information do I need to use?**
how many **beads** Ava has	the number of , ___○___ , ___△___ and ___□___ in the picture

Show how to solve the problem.

Color the first bar to show there are 4 circles.

Beads Ava Has						
circle ○						
square □						
triangle △						
	0 1 2 3 4 5 6					

Use the graph. Write how many. Add to solve.

1. __4__ ○ + __4__ □ + __2__ △ = __10__

How many beads does Ava have? __10__ beads

Name _____

Lesson 85
CC.1.MD.4

Use the bar graph to answer the question.

Coins Jared Has	
penny	
dime	
quarter	
	0 1 2 3 4 5 6 7 8 9

1. How many fewer pennies than dimes does Jared have?

○ 1   ● 2   ○ 3   ○ 4

2. How many dimes does Jared have?

● 8   ○ 6   ○ 5   ○ 3

3. How many more dimes than quarters does Jared have?

○ 1   ○ 4   ● 7   ○ 8

4. Look at the bar graph. Suppose Jared uses 3 dimes to buy a marker. How would the bar graph change?

Possible answer: The bar for dime would get shorter. It would go to 5, not 8. The bar for penny would be the longest.

Name _____

Lesson 86
COMMON CORE STANDARD CC.1.G.1
Lesson Objective: Identify and describe three-dimensional shapes according to defining attributes.

Three-Dimensional Shapes

curved surface	curved and flat surfaces	
sphere	**cone**	**cylinder**

flat surfaces

rectangular prism   **cube**

Color to sort the shapes into three groups.

1. only **flat surfaces** 🖍 RED — cube, rectangular prism

2. only a **curved surface** 🖍 BLUE — sphere

3. both **curved** and **flat surfaces** 🖍 YELLOW — cone, cylinder

cone   cube   cylinder

sphere   rectangular prism

Name _____

Lesson 86
CC.1.G.1

1. Which shape has **only** flat surfaces?

●   ○

○   ○

2. Which shape has both flat and curved surfaces?

○   ○

●   ○

3. Fred sees an object with **only** a curved surface. Which might be Fred's object?

●   ○

○   ○

4. Which shape has both flat and curved surfaces?

●   ○

○   ○

5. Write the name of the shape.

__sphere__

Answer Key

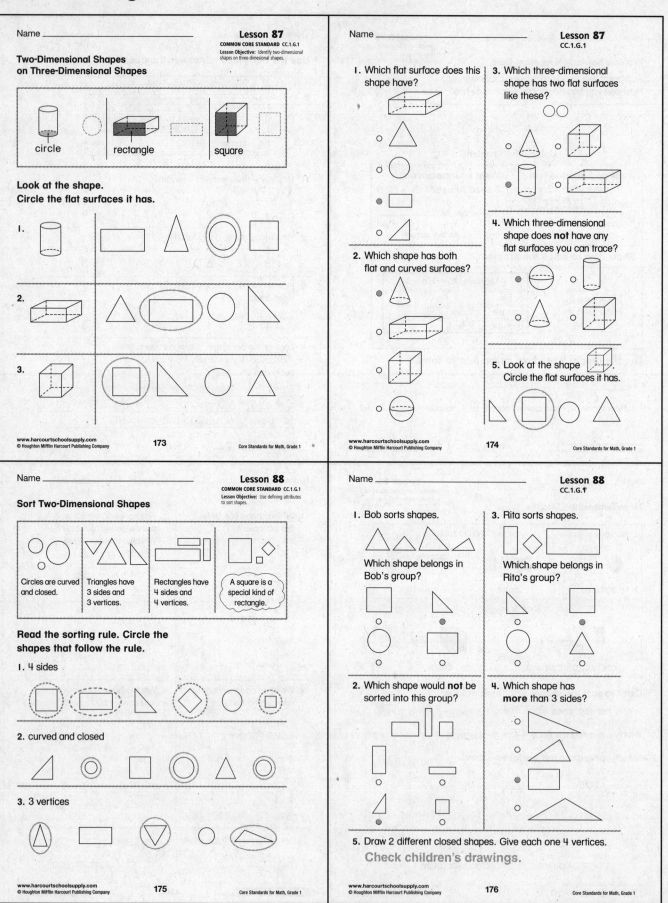

Answer Key

Name _____ **Lesson 89**

COMMON CORE STANDARD CC.1.G.1
Lesson Objective: Describe attributes of two-dimensional shapes.

Describe Two-Dimensional Shapes

side → [rectangle]

vertex

This shape has 4 straight sides and 4 vertices.

Write the number of straight sides or vertices.

1. triangle ___3___ sides

2. square ___4___ vertices

3. hexagon ___6___ vertices

4. trapezoid ___4___ sides

5. triangle ___3___ vertices

6. square ___4___ sides

www.harcourtschoolsupply.com
© Houghton Mifflin Harcourt Publishing Company
177
Core Standards for Math, Grade 1

Name _____ **Lesson 89**

CC.1.G.1

1. Which shape has 6 sides and 6 vertices?

○ hexagon ●
○ triangle
○ square
○ rectangle

2. How many straight sides does this shape have?

○ 1
○ 2
○ 3
● 4

3. Which shape has 4 vertices and 4 sides that are the same length?

○ triangle
● square
○ triangle
○ rectangle

4. Which shape does **not** have 4 sides?

○ square
○ rectangle
● triangle
○ trapezoid

5. Jed says that shapes cannot have curves. Is he correct? Draw or write to explain.

No. Check children's drawings or explanations; look for closed circles and ovals.

www.harcourtschoolsupply.com
© Houghton Mifflin Harcourt Publishing Company
178
Core Standards for Math, Grade 1

Name _____ **Lesson 90**

COMMON CORE STANDARD CC.1.G.2
Lesson Objective: Compose a new shape by combining three-dimensional shapes.

Combine Three-Dimensional Shapes

Put shapes together to make a new shape.

and do not make this shape.

Use three-dimensional shapes.

Combine.	Which new shapes can you make? Circle them.
1.	(circled) (circled)
2.	(circled) (circled)

www.harcourtschoolsupply.com
© Houghton Mifflin Harcourt Publishing Company
179
Core Standards for Math, Grade 1

Name _____ **Lesson 90**

CC.1.G.2

1. You have [cube] and [cylinder]. Which new shape can you make?

○ ○ ● ○

2. You have [cylinder] and [cone]. Which new shape can you make?

○ ● ○ ○

3. You have two [rectangular prisms]. Which new shape can you make?

○ ○ ● ○

4. Circle the shape that **cannot** be made from [shapes].

○ ○ ○ (circled)

www.harcourtschoolsupply.com
© Houghton Mifflin Harcourt Publishing Company
180
Core Standards for Math, Grade 1

---

www.harcourtschoolsupply.com
© Houghton Mifflin Harcourt Publishing Company

245

Core Standards for Math, Grade 1

Answer Key

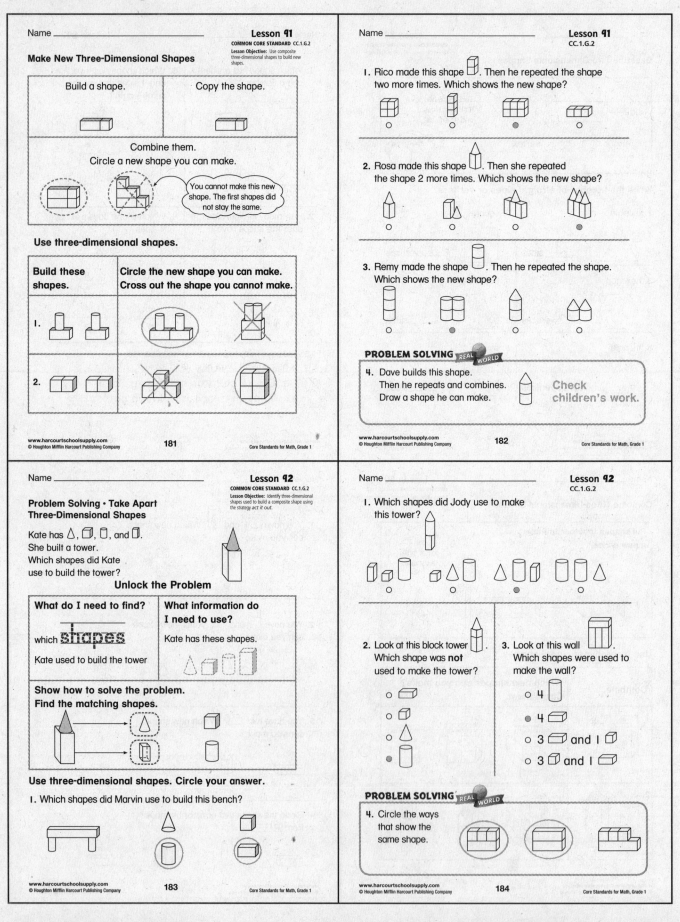

Lesson 93
Name _____

COMMON CORE STANDARD CC.1.G.2
Lesson Objective: Use objects to compose new two-dimensional shapes.

Combine Two-Dimensional Shapes

You can put shapes together to make a new shape.

3 △ make a ▽.

Use pattern blocks. Draw to show the blocks.
Write how many blocks you used.

1. How many ▽ make a ⬡?

___2___ ▽ make a ⬡.

2. How many ◇ make a ⬡?

___3___ ◇ make a ⬡.

Lesson 93
Name _____

CC.1.G.2

Use pattern blocks.

1. How many △ make a ◇?

1   **2**   3   4
○   ●   ○   ○

2. How many ◇ make a ⬡?

9   6   **3**   2
○   ○   ●   ○

3. How many ⬡ make 2 ⬡?

2   **4**   6   8
○   ●   ○   ○

PROBLEM SOLVING REAL WORLD

Use pattern blocks. Draw to show your answer.

4. 2 ⬡ make a ⬡.

How many ⬡ make 4 ⬡?

Check children's drawings.

___8___ ⬡ make 4 ⬡.

Lesson 94
Name _____

COMMON CORE STANDARD CC.1.G.2
Lesson Objective: Compose a new shape by combining two-dimensional shapes.

Combine More Shapes

Combine shapes to make a new shape.

2 Shapes	Combine	New Shape

Circle the shapes that can combine to make the new shape.

1.

2.

3.

Lesson 94
Name _____

CC.1.G.2

1. Guy has 2 ◺. Which shape can he **not** make?

○   ○   ○   ●

2. How many □ does it take to make this shape?

2   3   **4**   6
○   ○   ●   ○

3. Which shapes can combine to make this new shape?

○   ●   ○   ○

4. Draw a new shape you can make from these shapes.

Check children's drawings.

Answer Key

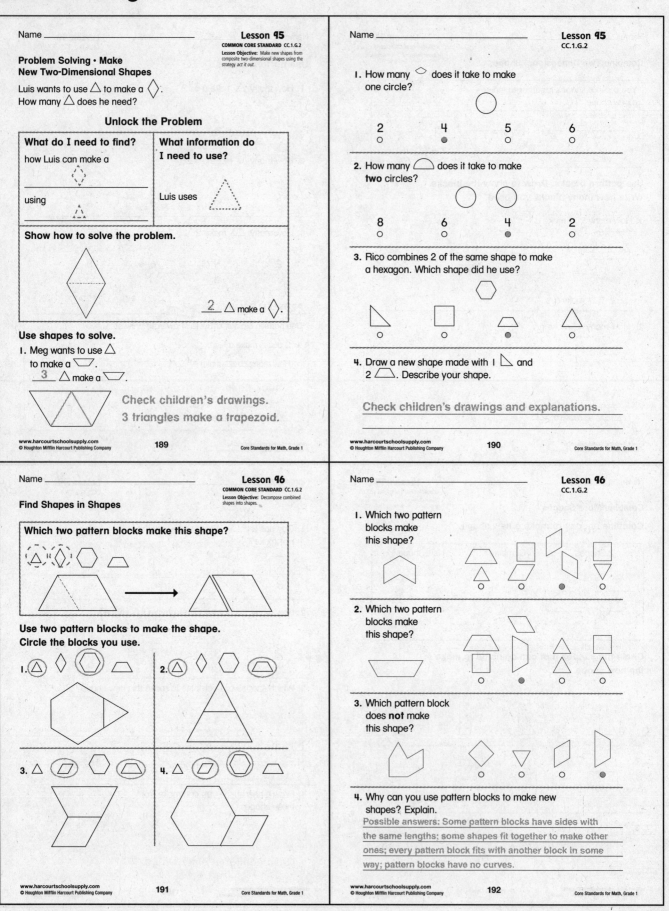

189

Core Standards for Math, Grade 1

Lesson 95

CC.1.G.2

190

Core Standards for Math, Grade 1

191

Core Standards for Math, Grade 1

192

Core Standards for Math, Grade 1

Answer Key

Name _____   **Lesson 97**
COMMON CORE STANDARD CC.1.G.2
Lesson Objective: Decompose two-dimensional shapes into parts.

Take Apart Two-Dimensional Shapes

Use pattern blocks to help you find the parts of a shape.

| Use 2 ▱ to find parts of ⬡. | Draw a line to show the parts. |

Use pattern blocks. Draw a line to show the parts.

1. Show 2 △.

2. Show 2 ▱.

3. Show 2 ▢.

4. Show 2 ⌓.

Name _____   **Lesson 97**
CC.1.G.2

1. Look at the shape. How many triangles are there?

   3 ●   4 ○   5 ○   6 ○

2. Look at the shape. What are the parts?

   ○   ● ●   ○   ○

3. Which shape can you make with 1 ▭ and 1 ▢?

   ○   ○   ●   ○

PROBLEM SOLVING REAL WORLD

4. How many triangles are there?

   4 small triangles.
   1 large triangle.

   ___5___ triangles

Name _____   **Lesson 98**
COMMON CORE STANDARD CC.1.G.3
Lesson Objective: Identify equal and unequal parts (or shares) in two-dimensional shapes.

Equal or Unequal Parts

| Equal Parts or Equal Shares (The parts are the same size.) | Unequal Parts or Unequal Shares (The parts are not the same size.) |

Circle the shapes that show equal parts.
Cross out the shapes that show unequal parts.

1.

2.

3.

4.

Name _____   **Lesson 98**
CC.1.G.3

1. Which shape shows **unequal** shares?

   ●   ○   ○   ○

2. Which shape shows **equal** shares?

   ○   ○   ○   ●

3. Which shape shows 4 **unequal** shares?

   ○   ●   ○   ○

PROBLEM SOLVING REAL WORLD

Draw lines to show the parts.

4. 4 equal shares

   Possible answers shown.

Answer Key

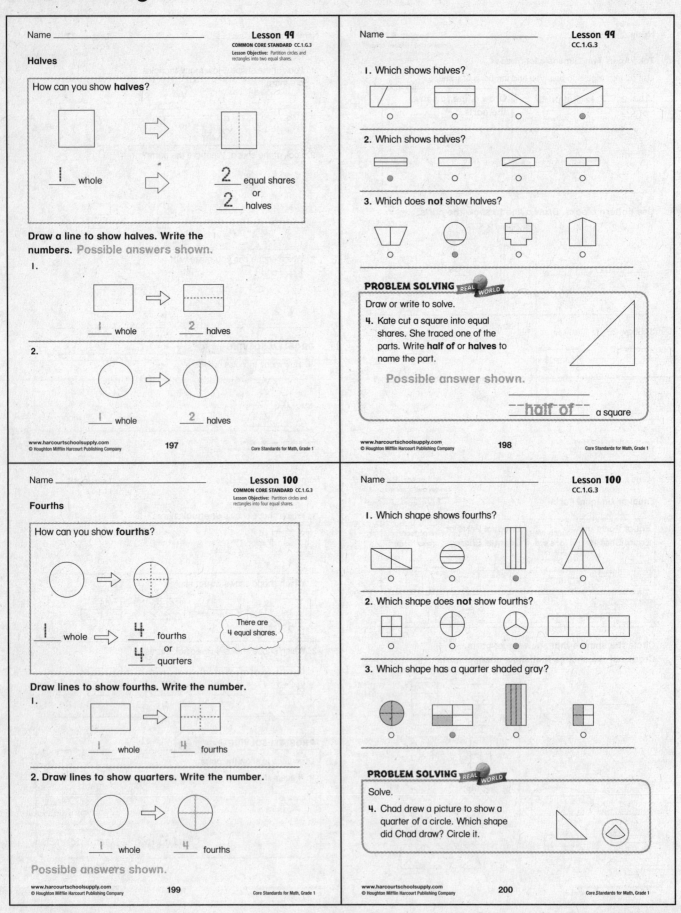

Halves

How can you show **halves**?

1 whole ⟹ 2/2 equal shares or halves

Draw a line to show halves. Write the numbers. *Possible answers shown.*

1.
1 whole   2 halves

2.
1 whole   2 halves

1. Which shows halves?
○ ○ ○ ●

2. Which shows halves?
● ○ ○ ○

3. Which does **not** show halves?
○ ● ○ ○

PROBLEM SOLVING REAL WORLD

Draw or write to solve.

4. Kate cut a square into equal shares. She traced one of the parts. Write **half of** or **halves** to name the part.

Possible answer shown.

half of a square

Fourths

How can you show **fourths**?

1 whole ⟹ 4/4 fourths or 4/4 quarters

There are 4 equal shares.

Draw lines to show fourths. Write the number.

1.
1 whole   4 fourths

2. Draw lines to show quarters. Write the number.
1 whole   4 fourths

Possible answers shown.

1. Which shape shows fourths?
○ ○ ● ○

2. Which shape does **not** show fourths?
○ ● ○ ○

3. Which shape has a quarter shaded gray?
○ ● ○ ○

PROBLEM SOLVING REAL WORLD

Solve.

4. Chad drew a picture to show a quarter of a circle. Which shape did Chad draw? Circle it.

Operations and Algebraic Thinking CC.1.OA

Represent and solve problems involving addition and subtraction.

1. Use addition and subtraction within 20 to solve word problems involving situations of adding to, taking from, putting together, taking apart, and comparing, with unknowns in all positions, e.g., by using objects, drawings, and equations with a symbol for the unknown number to represent the problem.

2. Solve word problems that call for addition of three whole numbers whose sum is less than or equal to 20, e.g., by using objects, drawings, and equations with a symbol for the unknown number to represent the problem.

Understand and apply properties of operations and the relationship between addition and subtraction.

3. Apply properties of operations as strategies to add and subtract.

4. Understand subtraction as an unknown-addend problem.

Add and subtract within 20.

5. Relate counting to addition and subtraction (e.g., by counting on 2 to add 2).

6. Add and subtract within 20, demonstrating fluency for addition and subtraction within 10. Use strategies such as counting on; making ten (e.g., $8 + 6 = 8 + 2 + 4 = 10 + 4 = 14$); decomposing a number leading to a ten (e.g., $13 - 4 = 13 - 3 - 1 = 10 - 1 = 9$); using the relationship between addition and subtraction (e.g., knowing that $8 + 4 = 12$, one knows $12 - 8 = 4$); and creating equivalent but easier or known sums (e.g., adding $6 + 7$ by creating the known equivalent $6 + 6 + 1 = 12 + 1 = 13$).

Work with addition and subtraction equations.

7. Understand the meaning of the equal sign, and determine if equations involving addition and subtraction are true or false.

8. Determine the unknown whole number in an addition or subtraction equation relating three whole numbers.

Common Core State Standards

Number and Operations in Base Ten

Extend the counting sequence.

1. Count to 120, starting at any number less than 120. In this range, read and write numerals and represent a number of objects with a written numeral.

Understand place value.

2. Understand that the two digits of a two-digit number represent amounts of tens and ones. Understand the following as special cases:

   a. 10 can be thought of as a bundle of ten ones — called a "ten."

   b. The numbers from 11 to 19 are composed of a ten and one, two, three, four, five, six, seven, eight, or nine ones.

   c. The numbers 10, 20, 30, 40, 50, 60, 70, 80, 90 refer to one, two, three, four, five, six, seven, eight, or nine tens (and 0 ones).

3. Compare two two-digit numbers based on meanings of the tens and ones digits, recording the results of comparisons with the symbols >, =, and <.

Use place value understanding and properties of operations to add and subtract.

4. Add within 100, including adding a two-digit number and a one-digit number, and adding a two-digit number and a multiple of 10, using concrete models or drawings and strategies based on place value, properties of operations, and/or the relationship between addition and subtraction; relate the strategy to a written method and explain the reasoning used. Understand that in adding two-digit numbers, one adds tens and tens, ones and ones; and sometimes it is necessary to compose a ten.

5. Given a two-digit number, mentally find 10 more or 10 less than the number, without having to count; explain the reasoning used.

6. Subtract multiples of 10 in the range 10-90 from multiples of 10 in the range 10-90 (positive or zero differences), using concrete models or drawings and strategies based on place value, properties of operations, and/or the relationship between addition and subtraction; relate the strategy to a written method and explain the reasoning used.

Common Core State Standards

Measurement and Data

Measure lengths indirectly and by iterating length units.

1. Order three objects by length; compare the lengths of two objects indirectly by using a third object.

2. Express the length of an object as a whole number of length units, by laying multiple copies of a shorter object (the length unit) end to end; understand that the length measurement of an object is the number of same-size length units that span it with no gaps or overlaps. *Limit to contexts where the object being measured is spanned by a whole number of length units with no gaps or overlaps.*

Tell and write time.

3. Tell and write time in hours and half-hours using analog and digital clocks.

Represent and interpret data.

4. Organize, represent, and interpret data with up to three categories; ask and answer questions about the total number of data points, how many in each category, and how many more or less are in one category than in another.

Common Core State Standards

Geometry

Reason with shapes and their attributes.

1. Distinguish between defining attributes (e.g., triangles are closed and three-sided) versus non-defining attributes (e.g., color, orientation, overall size); build and draw shapes to possess defining attributes.

2. Compose two-dimensional shapes (rectangles, squares, trapezoids, triangles, half-circles, and quarter-circles) or three-dimensional shapes (cubes, right rectangular prisms, right circular cones, and right circular cylinders) to create a composite shape, and compose new shapes from the composite shape.

3. Partition circles and rectangles into two and four equal shares, describe the shares using the words *halves*, *fourths*, and *quarters*, and use the phrases *half of, fourth of, and quarter of*. Describe the whole as two of, or four of the shares. Understand for these examples that decomposing into more equal shares creates smaller shares.